Where IS THE GOOD, God?

Where IS THE **GOOD,** *God* ?

FINDING GOOD IN OUR

GRIEF, SORROW, & DISAPPOINTMENT

KIM KISER

ISBN: 979-8-9920806-0-5

All Scripture quotations, unless otherwise indicated, are
taken from the King James Version. Public domain.

Scriptures marked NKJV are taken from the New King James
Version®. Copyright © 1982 by Thomas Nelson. Used by permission. All rights reserved.

Interior Design by Gloria Erickson, London Lane Designs

Cover Design by Julia Arambam

Published in the United States of America

Contents

Preface

My husband's death changed everything. Losing him rocked me to the very core of who I was and what I believed. Until this life-shattering event, I thought I knew exactly who I was and what I wanted out of life. I was secure in my identity as a follower of Jesus, a wife, and a mother. I was sure this identity was a firm foundation that would withstand whatever life might throw at me. I would be okay no matter what.

Nothing could have prepared me for what happened on November 2, 2014. What I knew in my head about security and identity shattered. I was alone, vulnerable, and scared.

This book is a compilation of ten years' worth of prayer, Bible study, and journaling. These things kept me grounded and able to move forward each day. Healing came gradually, and I knew that I wanted to share my journey with others. Writing a book seemed like the best way to do that.

We all have experienced loss of some kind. Grief and sorrow find us all, and disappointments can weigh us down. We have a picture of what we expect our lives to look like and what we need to feel safe and happy. When that picture gets smudged or shatters, we wonder what happened and what this means about who we are and what we believe. For me, this resulted in me feeling lost and alone and questioning every-thing about my identity. I knew God was there, but I questioned if I really knew Him. I had to reevalu-ate everything about myself and my faith. At first, I beat myself up with accusations of being weak and double-minded. And because I was accusing myself, I thought God was also accusing me. Turns out, that is not Who He is. Slowly, He reminded me of His never changing character. He reminded me that He is a merciful, gracious God who loves His children and understands our human condition. My thoughts and feelings were valid, and He wasn't waving a finger at me and shaking his head in disappointment. Instead, He was holding out His arms and seeing me with eyes full of love. He waited for me to let go of my self-protecting defenses and run to Him, my Father. Once I did, He reminded me of my true identity. He taught me that I felt lost and scared because I was building my life on the wrong things. Not bad things, just the wrong things.

I pray that this book draws you closer to God and reminds you of His perfect love. I hope it reminds you to face the storms and uncertainties in your life, remembering that God is still good and loves you. He's not displeased with you and frustratingly waiting for you to figure things out. He stands ready to comfort and love you.

Introduction

"Your husband's heart stopped on the operating table. We were able to get him back, but we discovered multiple blood clots in his lungs."

My whole world went dark. I could see the doctors talking, but I couldn't hear another word they were saying. Panic and fear gripped my heart, and I could only think that I needed to escape. I got up from the table and ran into the waiting room. I had to find help. Obviously, those doctors didn't know what they were doing!

Rob was admitted to the hospital the day before with shortness of breath. An examination revealed two heart blockages, which, they said, were causing him to have difficulty breathing. He would undergo a routine double bypass surgery, and we'd be on our way.

Within minutes after beginning the surgery, his heart stopped. They were able to bring him back, but now I was hearing words like *pulmonary embolism* and *cardiac arrest*.

No! This wasn't happening.

I wanted to disappear. I quickly scanned the waiting room for a hole, a pit. I ran to the end of the hallway and discovered the hospital chapel. Relieved to find it empty, I looked for the lowest place to retreat.

I fell on my knees and cried to God, "What is happening? Lord, please help us. They don't know what they're doing! We need you now. Please tell me what is happening."

The silence was deafening, and I was desperate for help. "Lord, please talk to me; show me what to do. Give me a word."

Looking up, I saw light streaming through the vaulted ceiling and the stained-glass windows. I was desperate to hear from God, but there was silence. I looked down at the Bible in my hand. Maybe God would speak to me through His Word. "Give me a Word, Lord," I prayed. With eyes closed, I opened my Bible.

"Jonah? Really, God? The story about the man getting swallowed by the fish?" Nevertheless, I said, "Okay, Lord. Speak to me." I looked down, and the verse that popped off the page was "Salvation is of the LORD" (Jonah 2:9). As if highlighted, that verse was all I could see.

Immediately, my heart rate slowed, the panic subsided, and I took a deep breath. "Okay, so that's the answer. You will save him. These doctors don't know what they're doing, but You do. Thank you, Jesus." After several more minutes of prayer, I returned to the room to talk with the doctors.

Have you ever considered that we are all just one accident, one diagnosis, or one broken relationship away from a shattered life? Moments like these may make us wonder where God is and if He really is good. Why did He let this happen? Why didn't He intervene, stop the perpetrator, heal the disease, or change the circumstances? Unbelievers may even mock us and say, "Where is your God now?"

I admit I struggled with God's goodness when I knew God could heal my husband yet didn't. After hearing Rob's prognosis, my whole world seemed to have turned upside down. Instantly, my sense of safety and security was pulled out from under me. It was like I was being pulled further and further out to sea without an anchor. Intellectually, I knew my faith should have been my anchor, but I did not feel steady or strong. Instead, I was terrified and unsure of what to do.

Fortunately, my faith did hold me together in those first days and weeks. Even though everything felt out of control and hopeless, I knew the One Who would help us, Who would save my husband. I knew He loved us and had all power to heal. We just had to wait and see what He'd do. He gave me His promise: Salvation is of the Lord. He would save my husband! I was confident He would put the pieces back together, and everything would be good again, just like before. Knowing this was the only reason I was able to walk out of the hospital chapel that day and into the next eleven days of ICU.

Answered Prayer

Walking through the halls of the ICU floor, I heard whispered conversations as doctors conferred with one another and saw family members, red-eyed and somber, standing outside the rooms. The sounds and smells reminded me that there were many gravely ill people there, and I prayed that God would show up and miraculously provide healing for all of them.

I don't know how the doctors and nurses managed the daily tension between encouraging families and relaying the truth of each patient's condition. On one day, my husband would be doing well and nearing the turning of a corner, and the next day, he would be the sickest individual on the floor. It was a rollercoaster I wanted no part of, but I found myself strapped in for the duration of the ride.

Then, just after midnight on a Sunday morning, Rob stood in the presence of his Savior. The Lord took him home. That verse returned to me: "Salvation is of the Lord." Yes, His promise held true, just not like I thought. God did save my husband. He took Rob to his forever home in Heaven, completely healed.

I know Rob is more alive and experiencing more joy and peace than he ever did here. The definition of salvation I interpreted in reading Jonah that day in the hospital chapel, however, pertained to his physical problems, saving his heart and his lungs so that he could walk out of the hospital and resume his life, our life. That's not how God saved him.

I realized then that God's plan and purposes aren't always obvious, and what I think is best does not always align with God's best. All I knew was that the pain I felt was intense and sharp. Physically, I felt tired and drained. My stomach hurt and felt tight. Emotionally, my heart was broken. The wind had been knocked out of me.

Walking, driving, and eating seemed to take so much effort. My world had stopped. The day he died was the darkest, most terrifying day of my life. How would I go on without him? What about the kids? Each of my children needed their father.

Our four boys, ages 11 to 17, said goodbye at the hospital. I would have to tell our three girls, ages four to nine, that their daddy wasn't coming home. That was the hardest thing I've ever had to do. Never have I felt so weak, so broken, but that's when I learned the truth of Jesus' words to Paul: "My grace is sufficient for you, for My strength is made perfect in weakness" (2 Corinthians 12:9). The supernatural strength that came from those words, from God Himself, is the only explanation for how I survived those first days, weeks, and months. It was His grace!

I'm sure you've heard someone say, or you've told yourself, "I don't know what I'd do if [fill in your worst-case scenario] happened." We've all seen others experience life-changing tragedies and decide we aren't strong enough to endure that. But one thing we forget in our imaginings is God's grace. He gives us the grace we need in the very moment we need it, not a minute earlier.

His strength was absolutely perfect in my weakness. When I have my own strength, I don't need His, but when I have no strength, there is abundant room for Him (2 Corinthians 12:9).

Although that day was the best day of Rob's life ("A good name is better than precious ointment; and the day of death than the day of one's birth" Ecclesiastes 7:1), it was the beginning of the hardest and darkest days of mine. I could survive only because we had built our lives on the solid foundation of Jesus Christ.

I wish I could say this faith made everything easy and smooth sailing. It didn't. However, it did keep me from drowning. The storm raged all around, and though I did not come out unscathed, I did come out standing (Matthew 7:24-27).

In the beginning, it was all I could do to function daily. I spent many hours praying for the pain to end. God carried me and comforted me. Never had I experienced God like I did in those days.

One night, after the house quieted, I lay in bed, weeping. The pain was intense, and I felt utterly alone. I just wanted to hear his voice again, to feel him next to me. I told God this as I prayed. Then, in the silence, I heard a man's voice say my name. I sat up in bed and looked around. No one was there. Strangely, it was comforting, not alarming. God heard me and answered me. Was it Rob's voice? Was it God's voice? I don't know, but the sound soothed me so I could fall asleep.

God gave me dreams, too.

One night, I dreamed of him sitting at his desk in

our room. In the dream, I woke up and thought, "Finally! You're here!" We had a great conversation, which allowed me to wake up for real and feel happy. Although the details of the dream faded quickly, preventing me from remembering the specific things we shared, just that we talked, I felt so much more at peace from having that final conversation.

This dream was comforting because we didn't have a chance to say goodbye. Throughout all the intense ups and downs at the hospital, I held on to that tiny sliver of hope that Rob would heal and come back to us. When he died, it happened quickly. I had questions to ask him, things I wanted to tell him.

Questions

Christians experience a supernatural peace beyond understanding when encountering difficulties and tragedies. God's promises and the hope of eternal life sustain us. Even though I had this faith, I was confused. I had so many questions.

If God is good and works all things for our good, how can leaving me a widow with seven children to raise ever work for good? Didn't God create the family with a mom and a dad? Isn't that the way it's supposed to be? Why would he take a good husband, father, and leader so early when he still had so much more to do?

I further wondered if it was "normal" for Christians to have such questions. Did my questions show a lack of faith? Did others have similar questions when faced with life-altering challenges and traumas? Indeed, I heard another widow say that a family member asked her, "Where is your faith?" as she was grieving and struggling.

Yes, others are watching to see if our actions match our words. In fact, I was wondering the same thing about myself! Did I have faith? Was I trusting God?

Come with me as I share how this journey led me to discover that my doubt, fear, and pain did not mean my faith was gone or false and how God did work all these things for good.

Rest assured, if we have faith as small as a mustard seed, it can grow beyond measure. In my weak state and with my tiny faith, I felt the strength of Jesus.

It is true: when we are weak, He is strong.

> Heavenly Father,
> Thank you for supplying us with Your strength and grace when we experience seemingly impossible circumstances. Thank you for being near when we are broken and offering comfort and peace that surpasses all understanding. You are perfect in all your ways and holy in all your works. We may not always see what You see nor understand what You are doing, but we can always trust You and depend on You, knowing that You are good.
> In Jesus Name,
> Amen

Chapter 1

Grief

Before Rob passed away, I fully trusted God's goodness and followed Him. He forgave me and chose me when I was still dead in my sin (Romans 5:8). Do you believe you are loved, chosen, and forgiven—not for anything you've done or could do, but because God loves you that much (Ephesians 2:8-9)?

I firmly believed that and still did after Rob passed; however, my pain and sorrow were so great that I felt God had rejected me. He had taken my best friend and partner in life. I needed many years to come to a place of healing and understanding that God did not reject me. God was then, is now, and forever will be the One

Who loves us most. He never changes and will never forsake His own (1 John 4:9-10; Deuteronomy 31:6).

One day, while teaching His disciples, Jesus said, "Verily, verily, I say unto you, Except ye eat the flesh of the Son of man, and drink his blood, ye have no life in you" (John 6:53). Many were confused and said, "This is a hard saying; who can hear it?" They thought He meant literally to eat His flesh and drink His blood. How shocking this must have sounded to them!

Of course, we now have the full Gospel, but they had no idea what Jesus would do or how His body would become the perfect sacrifice. Many of the disciples, except for twelve, turned and stopped following Him that day. Jesus asked those who remained, "Will ye also go away?" Simon Peter answered, "Lord, to whom shall we go? Thou hast the words of eternal life" (John 6:60-71).

I also wondered where to turn. I didn't understand why Rob had to die so young. Why were our children left to grow up without him? Why was I a widow after only 20 years of marriage? I didn't understand any of it, but I had nowhere else to go but to the Lord. He has the words of eternal life. However, knowing this did not diminish my grief.

An *American Dictionary of the English Language* defines grief as "the pain of mind produced by loss, misfortune, injury or evils of any kind; sorrow; regret."[1] It refers to the French word for grief, *grever*, which means *to oppress*. I would agree with this definition, but my grief felt more like the heavy weight of oppression. Oppress means "to load or burden with unreasonable impositions; to treat with unjust severity, rigor or hardship."[2] While difficult to put into words, the heavy weight I carried, along with the certainty it would crush me at any minute, more accurately describes how I felt after my husband passed than "pain of mind." The full weight of filling both roles of mother and father to my children seemed an unrealistic expectation. I felt alone and abandoned.

I had spent more of my life with Rob than without him. We met at a Christmas party just two weeks after my

17th birthday. I told my friend Christy there was something special about him, and I knew I had to get to know him. "Forget about it," she said. "He has a girlfriend, and you have a boyfriend!" So, I broke up with my boyfriend, and apparently, Rob felt the same way—he broke up with his girlfriend, too! We connected soon after, and our relationship began.

Early on, I knew he was the one I would marry. When I was with Rob, I felt I was home. I felt safe and loved. We dated through college, and despite having our share of ups and downs, life was easy and good when we were together. On December 10, 1993, almost six years after we met, Rob showed up at my apartment with a dozen roses and a ring. We married the next August, and I really was home. We were home.

Rob was a wonderful husband, father, protector, and provider. I never had to worry or do without anything. Then suddenly, I had to take on the roles of protector and provider for my kids with no one to provide for and protect me. I'd have an image of myself in a desert, alone and without shelter, exposed and vulnerable to the elements. The feeling tormented me throughout the day and in my dreams, too.

A few months after Rob passed, I had a dream where I was searching everywhere but couldn't find him. I woke up feeling defeated and rejected, smacked with the realization that I wouldn't find him. He was gone.

This same dream plagued me for about four years! Sometimes, months would pass before it would replay, but when it did, my unconscious mind would sense the dream coming on, and the dread of having to go through the experience again would cause my spirit to sink.

Each dream shared the same beginning but would vary in how I tried to find him. In one dream, I had the idea to call his mom. Surely, she would know where he was, but she didn't. And she didn't know his number either! I tried calling his friends in another dream, but no one knew where to find him. I'd feel like the worst wife for forgetting his phone number.

I wondered why he didn't try to contact me. Didn't he want to see me?

The rejection and abandonment didn't make sense to me. In fact, our hearts' emotions don't always match our brains' logical reasoning. Rob didn't reject us. He didn't choose to leave us. At the time, it didn't occur to me that I was feeling rejected and abandoned by God, not my husband. Thinking back, I believe my subconscious was protecting me from questions that seemed unfitting for a true Christian to ask.

I kept telling myself that everything happens for a reason. Just trust and don't have doubts or ask questions. On some level, I thought God would be angry if He knew how much confusion and hurt I felt. My questions would somehow show I did not trust Him or have true faith in Him.

Truth be told, God was all I had to cling to in those dark days. I felt unsure of who I was in this new life. Losing my husband felt like losing myself. My whole identity was wrapped up in him and our life together.

This makes sense if you consider that God calls married couples "one flesh." My flesh literally felt ripped off, and half of me was gone. I found myself unable to function like I used to. I had no interest in reading, knitting, baking, and homeschooling—the activities I so enjoyed. At first, I thought that once the shock wore off, I'd return to my normal self. I was wrong. I had truly lost myself.

"No one ever told me that grief felt so like fear."[3] This first sentence of C.S. Lewis' book, *A Grief Observed*, perfectly describes my feelings. I feared messing up my kids, being taken advantage of, and making decisions independently. I was afraid of not being protected and having to navigate through the ups and downs, stresses, and challenges of life without my best friend. It was all on me, an unbearable weight. That was how I felt, but it was far from the truth.

I wish I could say my healing came in a neat package, and here's a step-by-step guide to follow for anyone who is grieving. I wish I could present a specific timeline and an order to my healing for others to follow.

But I can't. My healing took many turns, sometimes two steps forward and one step back. Eventually healing did come.

Even though I felt crushed and forgotten, I knew God was my only hope. I clung to Him and spent many hours praying and searching the Scriptures. Reading accounts of how God worked in the lives of His people as they faced challenging circumstances and suffered great losses provided comfort.

Daniel spent six days in a den of hungry lions. It must have been terrifying, wondering each day if they'd finally get hungry enough to devour him!

Job lost all ten of his children, his wealth, and his health in a single day. Eventually, God restored all and gave him twice as much as before, but the miracles didn't happen overnight.

The Bible does not tell us exactly how long he suffered, but some scholars believe it could've lasted months or years.

In the middle of it, having no idea that anything would change, Job laments being born! "Why died I not from the womb? Why did I not give up the ghost when I came out of the belly" (Job 3:11)? Later, he says, "Wherefore then hast thou brought me forth out of the womb? Oh that I had given up the ghost, and no eye had seen me! I should have been as though I had not been; I should have been carried from the womb to the grave" (Job 10:18-19). Obviously, Job was in great pain, great heaviness.

Although David had a call to be king, he ran for his life with King Saul trying to kill him. He lived as a fugitive for 15 years. In the Book of Psalms, we read many songs about his pain, loneliness, and grief, such as Psalm 77: 1-9:

> I cried unto God with my voice, even unto God with my voice; and he gave ear unto me. In the day of trouble I sought the Lord: my sore ran in the night, and ceased not: my soul refused to be comforted. I remembered God, and was troubled: I complained, and

my spirit was overwhelmed. Selah. Thou holdest mine eyes waking: I am so troubled that I cannot speak. I have considered the days of old, the years of ancient times. I call to remembrance my song in the night: I commune with mine own heart: and my spirit made diligent search. Will the Lord cast off forever? And will he be favorable no more? Is his mercy clean gone forever? Doth his promise fail for evermore? Hath God forgotten to be gracious? Hath he in anger shut up his tender mercies? Selah.

David was in great pain, wondering if he would ever find relief. In the first few years of my widowhood, I sometimes wondered if I would ever feel whole again or if God even heard me.

When Lazarus got sick, his family's grief was great as they watched him grow weaker and weaker, yet Jesus did not come to help him before he died. They could not know what would happen in just four days when Jesus arrived.

Paul traveled to many different cities to proclaim the name of Jesus and spread the good news of the Gospel. What did he get in return? He was beaten with rods, received 40 stripes minus one, and stoned. He was shipwrecked three times "in perils of waters, in perils of robbers, in perils of my own countrymen, in perils of the Gentiles, in perils of the city, in perils in the wilderness, in perils in the sea, in perils among false brethren; in weariness and toil, in sleeplessness often, in hunger and thirst, in fastings often, in cold and nakedness" (2 Corinthians 11:27).

Whew! And I thought I had it hard! Paul was buffeted at every turn, yet he never gave up. Each time he narrowly escaped death, he would dust himself off and continue to the next city. He kept going and proclaimed the truth, no matter what the cost. Moreover, Paul saw a rather violent end in a martyr's death.

Naomi found herself alone in a foreign country after losing her husband and both of her sons. Naomi said, "The Almighty hath dealt very bitterly with me" (Ruth 1:20). Even though her daughter-in-law, Ruth, stayed by her side, Naomi felt forsaken and desolate. She lamented, "I went out full, and the LORD hath brought me home again empty" (Ruth 1:21). Her dreams for her life had been shattered, and she couldn't see any hope facing a future without her husband and sons.

Because I can read each of these individual's stories from beginning to end in one sitting, it is easy to gloss over just how much they suffered and lived through a time when all seemed hopeless. They endured many days, and sometimes years, of hopelessness and pain. I think about what it must have been like for them and how they managed their grief and sorrow. In our own lives, we only see what's directly in front of us. How amazing it would be to be able to look behind the curtain and see how our present circumstances will turn out! Of course, we can't, but we do have this vantage point in Scripture and can learn much from these ancient people. It's important to remember that, just like us, there was a time when these people felt hopeless and wondered if they would ever find relief from their suffering. They couldn't look behind the curtain either, but we have the privilege of seeing how God carried them and eventually delivered them. We serve and are loved by the very same God.

Come with me as I introduce you to four giants of the faith and what they teach us about living through difficult times of grief.

> Heavenly Father,
> Thank you for the Bible. Thank you for sharing testimonies of people just like us who walked through fiery trials and made it to the other side. Thank you for making Yourself known through these accounts so we can be encouraged in our walk. Life is often difficult and confusing, but we are thankful to know that You are there working for us, holding us, and making a way for us. We are grateful for your Word. Please guide us and teach us as we read it. We love you!
> In Jesus Name,
> Amen

Chapter 2

Investing in a Relationship with God

Shortly after midnight, November 2, 2014, Rob was gone. After several attempts to bring him back, the doctors said there was nothing else they could do. My sweet husband had transitioned to his eternal home, leaving all of us behind. I'll never forget how it felt to stand beside his bed and hold his hand. The full weight of the realization of what just happened hit me like a ton of bricks; he was truly gone. I felt like I was in someone else's body, someone else's story. This couldn't have just happened.

My sons and I somehow made our way to the parking garage, got into Rob's truck, and began the drive home. I remember feeling like everything was happening in slow motion, like we were moving through a very thick fog.

I hadn't been home in 12 days. Friends and family were so gracious and cared for our house and the children while we were gone. I was incredibly blessed to have been given the gift of being fully present with Rob during his last days. These same friends also brought the children to the hospital for visits. Although the girls did not go up to the ICU floor to see their dad, I was able to hug them and assure them that the doctors were doing everything they could to help their daddy. I decided it would be too traumatizing for them to see their dad with all the wires and tubes. They were still so young. Instead, the last memories of their dad would be the strong man who could hold all three of them at one time. The dad that sang and played with them.

We arrived home early that Sunday morning, and I

collapsed, exhausted, into bed. My whole body felt heavy as I opened my eyes later that morning. It took everything in me to get out of bed and get dressed. The silence in the house was deafening as I waited for the girls to come home. Before too long, the front door flew open, and three little girls bounded into the house, screaming with delight to find me there. Immediately, they began asking about their daddy. Where was he? When would he be home? Holding them tightly, I forced myself to say the words: Daddy's not coming home. He is in Heaven with Jesus. We all cried together for a long time. I tried my best to answer all their questions, but I could tell they didn't understand. I didn't understand it myself! The grief and sorrow felt like it was going to suffocate me. I wondered how I would survive.

Looking back, I am grateful for the investment I made in a relationship with Jesus. We typically think of investments in terms of money. Investing our money wisely prepares us for the unexpected expenses that life throws our way, such as a blown car engine or broken air conditioner. Similarly, investing time in drawing near to Jesus can yield huge dividends in life's unexpected storms. There is no doubt in my mind that it was the foundation I had built my life on that kept me from drowning. A life built on the Rock, on Jesus, is what carried me through (Matthew 7:25).

When all is right in our world, it is easy to praise and thank God. We are quick to say, "God is good," when a disease is healed, a surgery is successful, a baby is born, or a happy couple celebrates an anniversary. But what happens when the tough times come—when a loved one dies, or a marriage breaks up? This is when we need to pull from our stores of faith to remember that God is still good even though our circumstances are not.

Daniel

Daniel is a great example of how time invested in a relationship with God carries us through darkness and uncertainty. Even though he was a young boy when he was stolen from his home, Daniel's relationship with God sustained him.

When Babylon conquered the Kingdom of Judah, Daniel, along with many other Jews, were carried away as captives. The King of Babylon, Nebuchadnezzar, ordered Ashpenaz, the master of his eunuchs, to collect a group of children from the nobility of Judah, children "in whom was no blemish, but well favored, skillful in all wisdom, cunning in knowledge, and understanding science, and such as had ability in them to stand in the king's palace" (Daniel 1:4). Nebuchadnezzar wanted wise children to whom he could teach the language and ways of the Chaldeans, the people of Babylon.

Daniel and his three friends Hananiah, Mishael, and Azariah (whom Nebuchadnezzar renamed with Babylonian names—Belteshazzar, Shadrach, Meshach, and Abednego, respectively)—stood out among the other children because "God gave them knowledge and skill in all learning and wisdom: and Daniel had understanding in all visions and dreams" (Daniel

1:17). Nebuchadnezzar "found them ten times better than all the magicians and astrologers that were in all his realm" (Daniel 1:20).

Why did God give special favor to these four young men?

Daniel had been taken away from his family and thrown into a strange country and culture. We can only imagine how terrifying this must have been for him and all the young people. However, he did not let fear distract him from his devotion to and love for God. In fact, "Daniel purposed in his heart that he would not defile himself with the portion of the king's meat, nor with the wine which he drank; therefore, he requested of the prince of the eunuchs that he might not defile himself" (Daniel 1:8).

Why would eating the king's food defile him? It could be that the meat was unclean according to Jewish law, or it had been offered to their false gods as a sacrifice. Eating meat sacrificed to idols is a serious problem for Jews. And, although wine is not considered unclean, it, too, could have been used in a sacrificial ceremony. Another explanation could be that eating the food would represent accepting the king's friendship and patronage. This would imply loyalty and commitment to the Babylonians.

Daniel takes a stand here to keep his loyalty singular to the one and only True God. It took a lot of courage for Daniel to make this request—one that could've gotten him thrown into prison or killed. Daniel's convictions and love for his God were so deep that they outweighed the consequences he might face. Seeing such bravery and loyalty in a young boy is remarkable.

Accordingly, God went before Daniel, for it says that "God had brought Daniel into favor and tender love with the prince of the eunuchs" (Daniel 1:9). Daniel requested that he and his three friends be given "pulse" to eat and water to drink. Pulse refers to beans or seeds grown for food, a plant-based diet. The eunuch was scared, thinking the boys would grow weak and sick, as well as put him in danger—specifically, of losing his head—if the king saw what they were eating.

Daniel pleaded with the eunuch to give them just ten days. If they looked sickly compared to the other children who ate the king's meat, he could deal differently with them. The eunuch agreed.

Ten days later, the eunuch was astonished to find that "their countenances appeared fairer and fatter in flesh than all the children which did eat the portion of the king's meat" (Daniel 1:15). Daniel and his friends were allowed to continue consuming the pulse and water, never defiling themselves. In the face of a seemingly impossible situation, Daniel held onto his faith and stood firmly in staying true to his God. Daniel's close relationship with God strengthened him to endure those difficult days.

Later, as an old man, his relationship with the Lord and refusal to share his worship with anyone or anything else gave him strength to withstand six days in a den with hungry lions. Even though God did not remove him from his circumstances, He showed Daniel mercy and helped him through his trials.

I experienced this same mercy and help as I walked through my trial. About 12 years before Rob got sick, I began to walk with God intentionally. Prayer and Bible reading became my daily habit. Little did I know then that this time spent with the Lord was storing up crucial banks of strength and courage that I would need to draw on later. The time I invested over those years was indispensable when I began walking through my husband's illness and, later, his death.

Rob had many friends, and I was inundated daily with texts, calls, and emails from loved ones wanting to know how he was doing. A friend suggested I set up a Caring Bridge page to post updates. Posting updates on the site became more than just relaying facts about his condition. God's word filled my mind as I wrote and comforted me. Seeing how others were responding with thanksgiving and praise to God, I realized that my investment in time with God was coming back twofold: strengthening and comforting me and so many who were connected to Rob *and* me.

As we go through difficult ordeals, it is easy to question God. We wonder where He is and why He let this happen. The Bible doesn't mention the parents of the children who were taken captive, but as a mom, I can imagine the heartbreak and grief they endured from losing their sons and daughters to a Godless nation. How horrifying it must have been for them not to know their fate!

Further, we don't know if these mothers and fathers survived to see their children again. Daniel's parents probably had no idea of the way God would use him or the mighty man of God he would become. How could they? They may have even died before Daniel reached adulthood. They certainly never got to read the book of Daniel! But we get to read it and see where God was and why He let that happen.

In the present moment, we often cannot see the way God is working. Sometimes we feel like He's not there at all! How wonderful that we have the Scriptures to show us that He is always there. He never changes, and His promises are guaranteed. Through accounts like Daniel's, we can see the bigger picture, a view we don't have in our lives. Knowing this gives me peace of mind and hope in the perfect will of God.

David

David's story encourages us to remember that God is faithful with His promises, and we can be sure of His calling even in the waiting. His story also teaches how our calling can help us navigate through times of grief.

Have you ever heard the Lord calling you to a certain place, job, or ministry yet found that the conditions for it to happen were not unfolding? Waiting can make you doubt if such a call is from the Lord, especially if circumstances are such that you don't see a clear path in front of you and may even point you in the opposite direction. David was only 15 when God anointed him to be king over Israel. However, 15 years would pass, making David 30, when he finally took the throne.

David's call was clear because God told His prophet Samuel to anoint David as king. On a side note, although he was a prophet with direct access to God, Samuel did not receive the person's name to anoint. God told Samuel only that he would find the one who would be king at Jesse's house. Samuel had to rely on the Spirit of God to show him who it would be after he arrived at the location.

It's safe to say most of us do not get such a direct word from God! However, here was David, a young boy with no outstanding characteristics that would lead anyone to see how he would reign as a king, being anointed over Israel by a respected prophet of the Lord.

Have you ever felt the Lord leading you somewhere, yet you hesitated because you were unsure of what you'd say or how you would accomplish the mission once you got there? Samuel's experience is a good reminder to be willing and obedient to walk into whatever God calls us despite our uncertainties. God will provide. His timing and grace are perfect.

Often overlooked as the youngest of eight sons in his family, David wasn't considered strong enough to go off to war with his brothers when they were called to fight the mighty Philistine army. The Bible neither tells us what David thought about this new identity after Samuel had anointed him nor reveals what his family thought as they witnessed the event. We can imagine that they were confused and a little doubtful. David just didn't look much like king material at the time.

A similar happening can occur when God calls us to something new. It might be big, like a new career, or something seemingly less significant, like a call to minister to a family in our church. We may look at our skills and present circumstances and wonder, *What? Me? Oh no, Lord, you've got the wrong girl! I'm not this. I don't have that. Therefore, how could I ever do that?*

For me, this new calling to widowhood was sudden and unwelcome. I was ill-prepared and felt incapable of fulfilling this new role. David's story reminded me that although I felt this way, God would equip me to fulfill my purpose, but only in His timing. David walked through 15 years of uncertainty, darkness, and grief before he saw God's call come to fruition.

When Samuel anointed David as king, "the Spirit of the LORD came upon David from that day forward" (1 Samuel 16:13). The very next verse tells us that "the Spirit of the LORD departed from King Saul, and an evil spirit from the LORD troubled him" (1 Samuel 16:14). In turn, Saul's servants suggested he find a man "who is a cunning player on an harp: and it shall come to pass, when the evil spirit from God is upon thee, that he shall play with his hand, and thou shalt be well" (1 Samuel 16:16).

Approving of the idea, Saul told them to find such a person and bring him to the palace. One of his servants immediately thought of David and replied, "I have seen a son of Jesse the Bethlehemite, that is cunning in playing, and a mighty valiant man, and a man of war, and prudent in matters, and a comely (good-looking) person, and the LORD is with him" (1 Samuel 16:18).

Saul summoned David to his palace. Greatly honored by the invitation, Jesse, David's father, sent his son with an ass laden with bread, wine, and a kid to express his gratitude. Saul was so impressed with David that he asked Jesse to allow the boy to remain there to serve him as his armor bearer and harpist. We might expect David, having recently been told by God that he would be king, to resist being a servant in the palace. Instead, he humbly submitted.

Has this ever happened to you? You sense a direct call from God, yet you find yourself in a place opposite that call, questioning whether what you heard was really from God. Don't waver! David had to go through training to take on this role as king. God knew exactly what He was doing in those 15 years. David was wise to trust Him and walk into each opportunity and circumstance with an open heart and mind to learn everything he needed to know to be ready to fulfill God's call to be king.

One day, while David was on an errand to care for his father's sheep, Jesse asked him to take food to his brothers in the army's camp and return with news of how they were doing. The Israelites were at war with the Philistines. When David arrived, he heard the Philistine champion, Goliath, threatening the Israelite army. David watched as the soldiers cowered in fear and then fled in response to a shouting giant that stood approximately 9 1/2 feet tall.

David was infuriated by the threats and outraged that "this uncircumcised Philistine" would dare to "defy the armies of the living God" (1 Samuel 17:26). When David's words reached Saul, the king sent for him. David told Saul, "Let no man's heart fail because of him; thy servant will go and fight with this Philistine" (1 Samuel 17:32). Saul eyed David and immediately stated that this was a bad idea. David was just a boy. What chance did he have against a giant who had been a man of war from his youth?

David explained to Saul that he killed a lion and a bear that threatened his father's sheep, and defeating this

Philistine would be no different. David was certain that just as God delivered him out of the paws of these wild animals, He would also deliver him out of the hand of Goliath. David's confidence must have moved Saul because he allowed him to fight this Philistine champion.

Saul gave David his armor to wear for protection, but David knew that the gear was not for him. Instead, David took the weapons that he had experience using: a shepherd's bag with five stones, a sling, and his staff. David further knew he would defeat Goliath through the LORD Himself, saying, "I come to thee in the name of the LORD of hosts, the God of the armies of Israel, whom thou hast defied" (1 Samuel 17:45). And of course, David killed the giant and became known as a great man of war.

Saul took David back to his palace that day, no longer allowing him to return to his father's house. Saul's pride, however, turned to jealousy when the women emerged from the cities of Israel singing, "Saul hath slain his thousands, and David his ten thousands" (1

Samuel 18:7). From that day forward, Saul knew that the Lord had departed from him to reside with David.

Saul wanted to kill David, forcing the young hero into 15 years of hiding. A few different times, David had opportunities to kill Saul and take over as king, but he never did. David knew that God was the one Who set kings on their thrones and removed them (Daniel 2:21). God's call on his life kept him focused through the darkest times.

Do you think David woke up on certain days feeling exhausted, as if he just couldn't do it anymore? Do you think he experienced moments of doubt and wanted to quit? Do you think he ever felt tempted to find a way out, even if doing so compromised his values? He was human; I'm sure he confronted such challenges.

So, what kept him on the right path? Along with the identity and calling God placed on his life, he possessed a deep-rooted faith and love for God through a relationship that began and grew while he was a young boy tending sheep on a hillside. The investment

David made in those early years paid huge dividends during the scariest, most trying times of his life.

As you contemplate David's life, don't discount humble beginnings. Use those times to dig into God's word and to spend time with Him.

Several years ago, as a new mom and a new Christian, I started hearing from Him unlike at any other time. It was an exciting period; I was overwhelmed by how much I was learning about God and how He was moving in my life. But one day, while in prayer, I had a disturbing revelation that caused me to speak out: "Wait a minute, God. Why are you teaching me all of this? Why are you revealing so much to me about Who You are? Are You trying to prepare me for something difficult?"

I don't know why, but it suddenly hit me that maybe my new revelations and closeness to God were preparing me for when I'd need Him in a mighty way. Something extremely hard might be coming into my life. And, as a young mom, my thoughts spiraled down into something horrible happening to my children.

I found myself pleading with Him: "Stop revealing yourself to me if you're doing it to prepare me for something unimaginable, like taking my children from me." Looking back, I admit I sounded slightly over the top, but I couldn't control my thoughts. Nonetheless, in the very next moment, I was repenting: "I'm sorry, Lord. Please forgive me. I love this new relationship I have with You, and I love discovering all the truths You have for me. Please continue walking with me and revealing Yourself to me."

Still, I had the revelation that the foundation I was building with Him would serve me in the face of tragedy, and I feared going through whatever it might be. Little did I know that in twelve years, I would find myself in that very place, pulling from the stores of the investment I had made in my relationship with God. I'm so thankful I had that strong foundation for support; otherwise, I tremble to think how my life would have gone.

With a solid foundation and calling from God, David continued day after day. Granted, he suffered bouts of grief. We read in many of his Psalms how he cried out to God and wept in pain. "Who will rise up for me against the evildoers? Or who will stand up for me against the workers of iniquity? Unless the LORD had been my help, my soul had almost dwelt in silence" (Psalm 94:16-17). His strength came through his weakness and faith.

We, too, can grieve and feel deep sorrow yet still retain our faith and love for Jesus. As a matter of fact, it is during those times of great pain that our hearts are most pliable, and God can strengthen and build our faith.

Naomi

Naomi's despair presents such an example in the book of Ruth. After losing her husband and two sons, she laments, "Call me not Naomi, call me Mara: for the Almighty hath dealt very bitterly with me. I went out full, and the LORD hath brought me home again empty: why then call ye me Naomi, seeing the LORD hath testified against me, and the Almighty hath afflicted me" (Ruth 1:20-21)?

I can identify with the pain and rejection Naomi felt. Years earlier, Naomi's husband had moved his family to Moab because of a great famine in their hometown of Judah. The famine had ended, and now left alone, Naomi decided it was time to return to Judah. She instructed her daughters-in-law, Ruth and Orpah, to return to their families. Ruth refused and followed Naomi. This is significant because Judah was not only the place where Naomi's family lived but also where Naomi's God reigned. The people of Moab worshipped other gods, not the one and only True God.

Even though Ruth accompanied her, Naomi returned to Judah feeling defeated and alone. With all God had taken from her, leaving her in deep grief and sorrow, Naomi still followed after God and worshipped Him.

Think about how difficult this time was for Ruth as

well. Having lost her husband, she was now leaving her own family behind. She and Naomi were returning to Naomi's hometown with nothing. To survive, Ruth went to glean wheat from other people's farms, which meant working long hours outside every day to keep food on their table. She never complained and served her mother-in-law faithfully.

While Ruth was working in the fields, a wealthy landowner and Naomi's relative, Boaz, noticed her. He was impressed with her humility and strength and further respected her for her kindness to Naomi and how she kept herself pure by not chasing after men. Eventually, he asked her to marry him, and the fields that Naomi once begged in became her own.

Later, God blessed Naomi with a grandson through Ruth and Boaz. There was a time when Naomi thought she'd never receive the gift of grandchildren! Overjoyed by God's mercy and grace, she praised God, "Blessed be he of the LORD, who hath not left off His kindness to the living and to the dead" (Ruth 2:20).

Naomi and Ruth walked through some pretty dark and difficult days. They grieved mightily. But God wasn't done. He had so much more for them.

In Chapter 1, I mentioned a recurring dream I had for years after Rob passed away. Every time, I would wake up feeling sad, empty, and alone. No matter what else was happening in my life, this dream would send me back to that dark place. In April 2019, the dream replayed once more, but, that time, it ended differently. I found him! Rob answered his phone, and I exclaimed, "I need to see you!" He agreed.

We met at a park for a picnic. Younger, in our early 20s, we talked about our upcoming wedding and had a joyous conversation about our future. I can't describe to you how wonderful that dream was! Then, I heard a noise that nudged me out of my sleep, and the dream slowly drifted away. I tried so hard to remain in the dream, but I could feel myself being pulled out of it.

I woke up feeling different that time: light and happy! Rob had been excited to see me and eager for our life together! And I got to see him again! As of this writing, I have not had that dream again, but it was a turning point in my healing. God was delivering me from the hurt and rejection I was feeling. Literally and figuratively, I was finally coming out of a bad dream. Just like with Naomi and Ruth, I understood that God had more for me. Hope and joy began to return to my life!

The presence of grief does not equate to an absence of faith. Grief is a natural emotion that we all carry at some point. What we do with our grief determines our spiritual, emotional, and physical health. Just remember that God is faithful in hearing us and providing for us when we call out to Him, just as He did for Daniel, David, and Naomi.

Heavenly Father,
We live in a fallen world. We know we will walk through trials and grief. Thank you for the gift of faith that gives us hope through these times. Thank you for your faithfulness. Thank you for hearing us when we cry out to you. Thank you for these stories

of your children that instruct us and show us Who you are. We are so grateful for Your Word because it's through Your Word that we learn who You are and what You've done. We are so thankful to serve You, a mighty, holy, awesome God!

In Jesus Name,

Amen

Chapter 3

Mourn with Those Who Mourn

Have you ever shared your grief with someone and had them respond, "I know exactly how you feel. I lost my ..." as they go on to tell you of their pain and grief? I think we've all expressed ourselves in that manner at one time or another. It's a way of trying to comfort the other person by letting them know they're not alone—we were there, too.

Unfortunately, such acknowledgments can intensify the grief-stricken person's loneliness because the focus shifts from giving comfort to listening to someone else's loss. Sometimes, it can even become a competition of whose loss is worse. Listening and resisting the urge to share similar situations is important when people share their grief.

We want so much to help others that we attempt to come up with a reason or explanation for their pain. By giving a reason, we hope to make the situation better. Those attempts can backfire, creating more stress and grief. Also, let's be honest: we don't know why it happened. We "see through a glass darkly" (1 Corinthians 13:12). Sure, we can conjecture and philosophize, but at this moment, our friend needs a shoulder to cry on and love, not an explanation.

These well-meaning "explanations" were given to me frequently after my husband went to his eternal home. One instance that stands out was on a Sunday morning at church. A preacher had come to visit for a special service. He knew my husband and had many kind things to say about him. I always love hearing how my husband influenced or impacted people. Towards the end of the conversation, he expressed his condolences and sadness over what seemed to be a premature homegoing. With his beautiful wife standing next to him, he then went on to tell me about her battle with cancer and how close she came to death. He explained that her recovery was because God knew he couldn't live without her.

At first, I just stared at them in disbelief. What made him think I could live without Rob? Or that God thought I could live without him? And how did he know what God thought, and this is why she was healed? What we think and what God knows are not the same thing. His comment left me feeling like I wasn't close enough to or as in love with my husband as I needed to be since God knew I'd be okay without him.

I know that this was not what this gentleman was implying, but it was what I heard. At that moment, I was offended and upset by what seemed to be an incredibly insensitive comment. However, now I can look back and laugh. What a crazy comment to make! We all do this, don't we? We try to figure out why things happen the way they do and think sharing our answers will provide comfort. Only God can provide answers and reasons to comfort. We are better off sharing memories of their loved one and expressing how they impacted our lives, not trying to offer explanations.

As someone who has been on the receiving and giving ends of comfort, I can attest that both positions are extremely difficult. Knowing what to say is hard. We may think we understand what they're going through, but no matter how similar the situation may look compared to our experience, we all have unique circumstances surrounding our grief.

There are a staggering 11.8 million widows in the U.S. and approximately 2,800 are added every day.[4] Each one has a distinctively personal story. I was a stay-at-home, homeschooling mom with seven children under 17. Although you might find other widows in similar situations, no two families are exactly alike, and no two people grieve the same way. Sure, we'll share certain commonalities and stages of grieving, but we all process emotions differently. Therefore, it's important to give our loved ones the room to grieve in their own time and way and to not invalidate their pain by sharing our own. Another time and place might be appropriate for that, but only when they are ready.

Job

Job's friends exemplify what to do—and what not to do—when trying to console a grieving friend.

At the beginning of the book, Job rose early in the morning to offer sacrifices and burnt offerings for each of his children after their days of feasting. A prosperous, Godly man, he said, "It may be that my sons have sinned and cursed God in their hearts." Moreover, the Bible says, "Thus did Job continually" (Job 1:5). We can see Job's devotion and love for God and his great love for his children.

The Bible describes him as "the greatest of all the men of the east" because of his wealth (Job 1:3). He had 7,000 sheep, 3,000 camels, 500 yoke of oxen, 500 she asses, and many servants. Although he had great riches at his disposal, Job did not place trust in such things; he trusted in God. That is why he sacrificed on behalf of his children. Job's wealth couldn't save them; only God could. This is a great lesson for parents. It doesn't matter how much money or material things we give our children. What counts is how much we pray and intercede for them.

From a worldly perspective, Job had a pretty great life. He had everything anyone could ever want or need. From a spiritual perspective, he had a perfect relationship with God. However, in one day, he lost all his worldly riches. The Sabeans and Chaldeans came to slay Job's servants and steal his livestock. A fire descended from heaven to consume his sheep and the rest of his servants. A great wind from the wilderness then destroyed the house where his children were feasting and killed them all.

Can we even begin to imagine how shocking and unbelievable this was for Job and his wife? One minute, everything was fine, and the next minute, their world was turned upside down and shattered into a million pieces. It's difficult to fully grasp the scope of loss these two people experienced and the depth of their grief. How would we respond in a similar circumstance?

"Then Job arose, and rent his mantle, and shaved his head, and fell upon the ground, and worshipped, and said, "Naked came I out of my mother's womb, and naked shall I return thither: the LORD gave, and the LORD hath taken away; blessed be the name of the LORD. In all this Job sinned not, nor charged God foolishly" (Job 1:20-22). Job's acknowledgment of God's sovereignty was an act of worship. Even with this overpowering grief, Job acknowledged that God had given him wonderful gifts and taken them away. And, in that, he blessed the Lord. Job's trust in God was not shaken. He maintained his faith and chose to believe that God was still the same God He had always been.

What about Job's wife? She said, "Dost thou still retain thine integrity? Curse God, and die" (Job 2:9). Job and his wife experienced the same magnitude of grief, but how they dealt with it was completely opposite. Job worshipped. His wife blamed God and suggested that Job just give up and die. Job's grief was mixed with hope. Job's wife's grief was mixed with fear. Fear is a liar and makes us think we're alone and vulnerable. Hope reminds us that we are never alone, and that God is always with us.

I must admit, there have been times when I felt like God had abandoned me, and I was ready to give up. I'm so thankful for testimonies like Job's to remind us that no matter our circumstances, God never changes. He is just as good in the tough places as He is in the wonderful places.

Next, as if Job had not suffered enough, he lost his health! He was stricken with "sore boils from the sole of his foot unto his crown. And he took him a potsherd to scrape himself withal; and he sat down among the ashes" (Job 2:7-8). "Despite everything, Job did not sin with his lips" (Job 2:10).

Most of us can relate to Job's reaction of shaving his

head and sitting among the ashes. His grief and sorrow were great, as were mine. There were many days when all I wanted to do was sit in my closet and cry.

Job had three good friends who traveled far to be *with* him, but what could they do *for* him? It's especially hard to know how to help if we have never experienced grief. Choosing the right words and actions can be difficult even when we have endured something similar. Nevertheless, as soon as Job's friends Eliphaz, Bildad, and Zophar heard what happened, they headed straight to his house to mourn with him and comfort him. Their example is a good lesson; our friends need us to show up.

Upon arriving, the three friends were shocked. They almost didn't recognize Job! His condition was worse than what they had heard. They all tore their clothes, sprinkled dust on their heads, and sat on the ground beside Job without saying a word. For seven days straight, they sat mourning with him in silence.

Simply sitting with them in their pain is probably

the best way to support and love those who are grieving. Our presence and compassion can be extremely comforting. So many of us are uncomfortable with silence, however. Compelled to fill in the space, we may say unfruitful or even damaging things. Job's friends understood and waited for him before offering any words of encouragement.

After seven days, Job spoke his first words: "Let the day perish wherein I was born, and the night in which it was said, 'There is a man child conceived.'" (In other words, *I wish I was never born!*) "Let that day be darkness; let not God regard it from above, neither let the light shine upon it. Let darkness and the shadow of death stain it; let a cloud dwell upon it; let the blackness of the day terrify it" (Job 3: 3-5). He further expressed a wish to die: "Wherefore (Why) is light given to him that is in misery, and life unto the bitter in soul; Which long for death, but it cometh not; and dig for it more than for hid treasures; Which rejoice exceedingly, and are glad, when they can find the grave" (Job 3: 20-22)?

Once Job broke the silence, his friends took turns addressing him. Unfortunately, this is where the good comfort stopped. They tried to explain why everything happened, stating it must be God's punishment for some evil that Job had done. Did they know of anything? No! But the explanation sounded plausible to them. Of course, their supposition was inaccurate. Job was upright, and he loved God.

Job and his friends did not know that Satan was the one who wreaked all the havoc. Satan told God that Job was a faithful man only because God put a hedge of protection around him and gave him great riches. Satan suggested that if all of that were taken away, Job would turn from God. God allowed Satan to take away all Job had, but when Job stayed faithful, Satan decided that ruining his health would be the final straw to break Job. That tactic didn't work either. While left in great misery, Job remained faithful.

The friends had no knowledge of Satan's involvement. We, too, don't always see the full picture. Speculating the reasons for a tragedy, accident, or other event is never good. We need to ask God, not lean on our own understanding (Proverbs 3:5-6).

Job's friends also tried to convince him to stop lamenting and cheer up—another poor idea.

Sometimes, well-meaning friends and family tell us it's time to stop grieving and move on with our lives. We may even tell ourselves this. If the sadness continues, we might feel our faith isn't as strong as we thought. Nothing could be further from the truth!

God wants us to confess our deepest thoughts and feelings. Our God-given emotions are valid. We need to acknowledge them, but we do not need to let them rule us. Recognizing and expressing our emotions is not only okay but important. Otherwise, we push them down, and unexpressed, repressed emotions don't disappear. They resurface in unhealthy ways. Symptoms of repressed emotions include physical sickness, angry outbursts, and impatience with others. Repressed emotions can further become strongholds that block our ability to see and hear God.

Confession is essential for healing. We see this throughout God's Word. Beginning with Adam and Eve, God knew exactly what they had done, but He still required them to tell Him. Confession is cleansing. God already knows the secrets of our hearts; just because we're hiding things from ourselves does not mean we are hiding them from God.

For our own good, we must release our concerns, including our doubts about Him, to God. He can take it. He's God! Surprised by nothing and infinitely strong, He can withstand anything we throw at Him.

When I finally realized this, I cried out to God, revealing all my dark feelings and faithless questions to Him. Surprisingly, I felt an overwhelming sense of peace and acceptance instead of shame or condemnation for admitting such things. I felt His love and care more strongly. I truly felt Him holding me and crying with me. Without question, "There is no condemnation to those that are in Christ" (Romans 8:1).

Towards the end of the chapter, Job wanted a full

explanation from God. Why did all of this happen to him? Perhaps hearing his friends speculate on the reasons for Job's great suffering led him to admit that he, too, wanted to know why. The answer rocked Job and reminded him of God's great power and sovereignty. God said Job did not have sufficient knowledge about the universe's complexities—how God created them or how He kept them going. God expected Job to trust His wisdom and character. Humbled by God's words, Job immediately repented. He acknowledged the majesty and mystery of God and apologized for speaking out of ignorance.

The book ends with God chastising Job's friends for their prideful explanations over things they knew nothing about. He said Job spoke rightly about Him, unlike Eliphaz, Bildad, and Zophar. Thus, although God did not approve of everything Job said, He appreciated Job's honest confession of his pain and emotions. This is prayer.

God instructed Job's friends to gather seven bullocks and seven rams for a burnt offering and said, "and my servant Job shall pray for you: for him will I accept: lest I deal with you after your folly, in that ye have not spoken of me the thing which is right, like my servant Job" (Job 42:8). Later, Job's family, friends, and acquaintances came to share a meal and comfort him. They also brought him "a piece of money, and every one an earring of gold" (Job 42:11).

Their gestures remind me of how we reach out to those suffering. We like to bring food and thoughtful gifts!

Last of all, God restored everything Job lost and then some! He gave Job ten more children—seven sons and three daughters. (And no women were deemed more beautiful in the land than Job's daughters.) He restored double the original number of each kind of animal he had lost. "So Job died, being old and full of days" (Job 42:17). Job lived to be 140 years old and saw his sons and sons' sons—four generations.

It's important to remember that everything was not immediately restored to Job. He lived many days, months, and years before seeing this reward. But, through it all, he stayed faithful to God and trusted His wisdom and goodness. Job's story reminds us that God is with us, although our present circumstances may seem dark and impossible. While we may not understand why these things are happening, we can trust in a good God and His perfect will.

When confronted with great loss and sorrow, we can grieve and cry out to God while continuing to bless and worship Him. God wants us to sacrifice everything to Him, including any strength or wisdom we think we have. He desires us to come to Him empty, ready to be filled with His strength, grace, love, and wisdom. This is the sacrifice of praise and true worship: admitting that we have nothing and God has everything we will ever need.

My assumptions are easy to make regarding the way God delivered Daniel, David, Naomi, and Job, who were serving God. In my life, though, I'll struggle not to question *why* upon seeing a Christian walk through devastating and traumatic circumstances.

We tend to think that if we're living for God, advancing His Kingdom, and praising and worshipping Him, He'll save us from traumatic situations, and life will be easy and good. However, it's obvious from these accounts and many others in Scripture that hardships and difficulties are part of a life set apart for Christ. As a matter of fact, Peter tells us not to be surprised by these trials, as though something strange was happening to us (1 Peter 4:12). If we live for Christ, we will face opposition, just as Christ did when He walked the earth. Ephesians says we wrestle not against flesh and blood, but against principalities, against the rulers of the darkness of this world and against spiritual wickedness in high places (Ephesians 6:12). Satan is always on the prowl, seeking whom he may devour (1 Peter 5:8). The very fact that we are following Christ immediately puts us in opposition with Satan. We are to rejoice and be glad that we can partake of Christ's sufferings because that is when His glory is revealed in us (1 Peter 4:13).

Neither Paul nor any of Jesus' apostles had it easy, but

they persevered in their calling to spread the gospel and further God's Kingdom amid trials and suffering. We don't follow Jesus in the hopes that we will never experience heartache and disappointments. We follow Him because, as Peter said, He has the words of life. He is the true source of joy and peace.

Stay with me, and I will show how God uses our deepest sorrows and toughest trials to make us look more like His Son and prepare us for our eternal home.

Heavenly Father,

Thank you for your unchanging nature and goodness. Thank you for your promise never to leave us nor forsake us. We can be confident that no matter what we experience on this side of heaven, we have a Father who loves us deeply and will carry us through our darkest valleys. Your ways and thoughts are so much higher than ours, so there is no way we will ever fully understand everything that goes on in this life, but we trust You. We will look to You continually and we eagerly anticipate the day when we see as we are seen.

In Jesus Name,

Amen

Chapter 4

Faith

Watching my husband lie in that hospital bed was excruciating. Was he in pain? Did he know what was going on? Was he scared? I felt helpless and hopeless. I couldn't understand why this was happening and was desperate to know if he would be okay. I had faith in God, but it seemed fragile and unstable.

Have you ever noticed that it feels the weakest when we need our faith the most? Here's the paradox: our faith has the most opportunity to grow at these times! When we can see the outcome, faith is unnecessary. It's only when we don't see that our faith comes into play.

What is Faith?

Faith is "the substance of things hoped for, the evidence of things not seen" (Hebrews 11:1). Faith believes that certain things are true when we don't see them. You've probably heard or read the expressions on plaques: *Faith over Fear* and *Faith>Fear* (faith is greater than fear). I think this is why I was questioning the strength or even the existence of my faith when my husband was in the ICU. I was scared. If I had faith, I wouldn't be afraid. If I was afraid, I must not have faith. I now know that neither one of these things was true.

Going into this trial, I had a strong faith in God. Scripture says faith is a "gift of God, not of works lest any man should boast" (Ephesians 2:8-9). I'm unsure of when I received my gift of faith because I have believed in God for as long as I can remember. I began reading my Bible daily when I started to walk by my faith. I wanted to know more about Him and to please Him—not because I feared what He'd do if I didn't, but because I was grateful for His love. I wanted to reciprocate that love. Subsequently, I was more active in pursuing and sharing Him with others. I began to understand the Bible in a way I never had before as the Holy Spirit revealed truth to me. I also saw evidence of His presence in answered prayer.

My family witnessed a miraculous answer to prayer when my son Brice was about six years old. He and his three brothers were playing in the woods behind our house. I couldn't see them, but I could hear them playing. Brice emerged from the woods and walked to where I sat on the back deck. The first thing he said was, "I fell." I couldn't see anything on his arms or legs, so I asked him if he was okay. He said, "I think so."

"Where did you fall?" I asked.

He explained that he tripped and landed on a pole when they were running through the woods. Confused because I didn't see any marks on him, I asked where the pole hit him. Without saying a word, he lifted his shirt, revealing a hole about the diameter of my thumb in his abdomen. The "pole" had impaled him! It wasn't gushing blood, but let's just say I almost fainted.

Picking up my baby girl, Rebecca, I rushed Brice over to my neighbor—a fireman across the street—for his opinion on what I should do. He immediately sent us to the emergency room. There was no way to tell how deep the puncture was, and it could have nicked his intestine. That would be serious. I was terrified. I left my other children with our neighbors and headed to the emergency room. As we drove, Brice's complexion turned pale, and he was trying to fall asleep. I prayed and cried the whole way to the hospital, begging God to spare my son.

To make a long story short, we left the emergency room a few hours later with a band-aid and an anti-biotic prescription. No damage to his internal organs! This seemed unbelievable as he had fallen onto a metal property stake, but the CT scan showed that it missed his intestine.

Later, I learned that Brice had walked out of the

woods alone because his three brothers had remained behind to pray at the spot where he had fallen. They were scared, but they knew the One Who could help. We were all fearful, yet our faith was still there. We believed in a miracle-working, life-saving God and knew how to run after Him.

I believe God heard our prayers that day. Answered prayers, where we see amazing healing happen, tend to strengthen our faith. God heard us, and He provided what we had hoped for.

Why did He answer our prayers? Was it because He heard our desperate cries and wanted to help us? Or was it because He had a greater purpose for Brice or possibly that incident? I don't know. All I can confirm is immense relief and gratitude flowed through me to know my son was okay.

Years later, there I was, in a hospital room with my husband's life in peril. Did I know the One I could run to for help? Of course. Did I have faith that God could heal him? Yes. Did I know for sure that He would return home with us? No.

Our faith is only as strong as the object of our faith. My faith was in God, not the doctors. The doctors had one desire and purpose: to heal Rob's heart, lungs, and blood so that he could walk out of the hospital and resume his life. Did they have the power to do this? Maybe. Did God have the power to do this? Definitely! But I knew enough about God to realize that I wouldn't always anticipate His plan or recognize His purpose.

Was it God's will for Rob's health to be restored? I had no idea because the Bible doesn't teach that God will always heal the sick to prevent death. As a matter of fact, it teaches just the opposite. The Scriptures tell us that we all will die. Our days are numbered from when we are fearfully and wonderfully made in our mother's womb (Psalm 90:12, Psalm 139:14).

God knew my heart desired to see Rob recover and return to us. However, I knew that it wasn't all about me and that His perfect will is not always clear to us.

If only we could see the end from the beginning as our Creator does. Maybe then, we'd understand.

Jonah

That first day in the hospital chapel, God showed me Jonah 2:9—Salvation is of the Lord—and the book of Jonah became precious to me after that. I read it many times in the months after Rob died.

Jonah exemplifies how relying on feelings and a self-focused attitude can lead us away from God. God gave Jonah a direct command to travel to Nineveh and warn the Ninevites of God's coming judgment. Nineveh, the capital of Assyria and one of the largest cities in the world at that time, was known for its cruelty and violence (Nahum 3:1-4). Jonah hated the Ninevites and did not want to warn them. He thought these people did not deserve a warning because of their despicable ways. They deserved to be annihilated off the face of the earth! It made no sense to Jonah why God would give them the time of day.

So, he hopped on a ship traveling in the opposite direction. Of course, hiding from God is impossible. God sent a great wind and storm that almost sunk the ship. The mariners were afraid and started unloading as much merchandise as possible to prevent the boat from sinking. The ship's captain decided to cast lots to find out why this terrible storm came up so suddenly. The lot fell upon Jonah.

Jonah explained that the Lord sent the storm because of Jonah's disobedience. He instructed them to throw him overboard to appease God's wrath and settle the storm. At first, the captain did not want to do this but finally consented. As Jonah said, the storm stilled, and the men were safe. However, God did not desire for Jonah to perish that night. Instead, He sent a giant fish to swallow up Jonah. While spending three days and three nights in the belly of this fish, Jonah cried out to God, praising Him for saving him from a watery grave.

"I cried by reason of mine affliction unto the LORD, and he heard me; out of the belly of hell cried I, and thou heardest my voice. For thou hadst cast me into the deep, in the midst of the seas; and the floods compassed me about: all thy billows and thy waves passed over me. When my soul fainted within me I remembered the LORD: and my prayer came in unto thee, into thine holy temple. But I will sacrifice unto thee with the voice of thanksgiving; I will pay that *that* I have vowed. Salvation is of the Lord" (Jonah 2:2-3, 7,9).

Notice how Jonah does not repent for running away. He doesn't tell God he's sorry or that he will go and do what God said if He'll let him out of the fish. But Jonah does shout praises and thanksgiving for saving him from the "billows and waves" that passed over him.

I can relate to these verses. When I first realized the grave danger my husband was facing, I felt like I had been thrown into a pit where I couldn't breathe. And just like Jonah, I cried out to God. He heard and reminded me of Jonah's words, "Salvation is of the Lord."

Have you ever heard God calling you to do something but weren't sure if it was really His voice you were hearing? If Jonah was unsure if the command to go to Nineveh was from God before, he could be certain it was after this miraculous encounter. Once on dry land, Jonah again heard God's command to go to Nineveh to preach God's warning. This time, Jonah obeyed.

Jonah's warning made an impression on the king of Nineveh. He got up from his throne, removed his robe, covered himself with sackcloth, and sat in ashes. He proclaimed a fast for every man and beast and commanded them to cover in sackcloth and cry mightily to God for forgiveness. He decreed that everyone must turn from their evil ways and violence.

God was pleased with their efforts and repented from the evil He planned. Nineveh was saved!

Here, we see Jonah's true heart. He still hated them. He was angry that God changed His mind. He wanted these people to get what they deserved: destruction. God had other plans. Jonah did not consider or care about these other plans. All he knew was that it didn't make sense; it wasn't fair.

Ouch! Does this sound familiar? It does to me. I'll see injustices around me and grow angry with God, whether it is something bad happening to an innocent person or a person or group of people getting away with evil. Maybe I am biased against a group, as Jonah was against the Ninevites. My views may be well-founded, but am I to be the judge and juror? Am I the one to decide exactly what should happen?

In His famous sermon on the mount, Jesus said, "Judge not, that you be not judged. For with what judgment you judge, you will be judged; and with the measure you use, it will be measured back to you. And why do you look at the speck in your brother's eye but do not consider the plank in your own eye" (Matthew 7:1-3 NKJV)? Jesus wants us to pay more attention to what's going on in our own hearts and work on those things than on the hearts of others.

We can't see what's happening in another person's heart anyway; only God can (1 Samuel 16:7). When I find myself forming judgments, I'm reminded of Jesus' words and Who He is. He is perfect in all His ways and holy in all His works (Psalm 13:30). He knows all, sees all, and is all-powerful (Psalm 115:3, Isaiah 55:11, Jeremiah 32:17). We can't always *understand* what He is doing, but we can always *trust* in what He is doing. Our grumbling and bad attitude will neither serve us nor those around us.

This next part of the story makes my heart rejoice, reminding me that God will never give up on us. God shows great patience and love in dealing with his wayward son. We may be wayward and stubborn at times, but He will always gently correct and guide us back to Himself.

In the final chapter, Jonah prays, "Ah, LORD was not this what I said when I was still in my country? Therefore, I fled previously to Tarshish; for I know that You are a gracious and merciful God, slow to anger and abundant in lovingkindness, One who relents from doing harm. Therefore now, O LORD, please take my life from me, for it is better for me to die than to live" (Jonah 4:2-3 NKJV)! In other words, "I knew it! I knew you were going to be merciful, and that's why I didn't want to come. Just kill me now!"

It's easy to look down on Jonah, but if we're honest, how often do we act this way? God does not perform as we thought He should, so we stamp our feet and throw a tantrum! God asked Jonah, "Is it right for you to be angry" (Jonah 4:4)?

Jonah did not answer God's question. Instead, he left the city and constructed a shelter to sit under to watch what would become of Nineveh. God then prepared a plant (gourd) to grow next to him to provide shade to ease his misery. Jonah was grateful for the plant and enjoyed the shade it provided. The next day, God sent a worm to damage the plant. It withered away. Then He sent a vehement east wind, and the sun beat down hot on Jonah. He grew faint and lamented, "It is better for me to die than to live" (Jonah 4:8). He then answered God's previous question by saying, "It is right for me to be angry, even to death" (Jonah 4:8)!

Talk about self-centeredness! It was all about Jonah!

First, he desired to run from God to avoid His command, and then it was his opinion of what should happen to the Ninevites—not God's desire or thoughts. He was grateful for the gift of the gourd and then angry when God took it away.

I can see myself in Jonah. I want life to be what I want, and I want God to respond a certain way to me and others. When the results I want don't happen, I grow sad, angry, or both!

Nevertheless, the Ninevites were important to God. He had a purpose for them, just as He had a purpose for Jonah. God also had a purpose for my husband, and there's no way I could know His intricate plans for Rob. I had plans for Rob, too, but I'm not God! God holds all our lives in the palm of His hand, and honestly, I wouldn't want my family or me to be anywhere else. What a paradox! Ultimately, I had no choice but to rest in the great wisdom of God and follow Him no matter where the path would lead.

Did I see it all this clearly at that moment? Absolutely

not! I prayed with everything I had for healing and for my precious husband to be returned to us.

Ultimately, I retained my strong love for and reliance on God in that dark valley because I trusted His infinite wisdom and pure love.

God asked Jonah a question at the end, which hints at a reason for His mercy. Later in Scripture, we read that God's judgment eventually came down on Nineveh. God purposed, however, that it would not be at this time. I encourage you to read the Book of Jonah. It's short enough to cover from start to finish in one sitting.

Recently, I heard a testimony of a woman trapped underwater for over 30 minutes and lived to talk about it! She claimed to have met Jesus in that place and recounted her feelings of great peace and love. Rather than being scared, she felt safe because Jesus was there. She witnessed a small piece of Heaven and learned that death wasn't the end but the beginning of a perfect life with our Creator.[5]

She wrote a book about her experience and took her youngest son to celebrate the day she finished her manuscript. On the way to the ice cream shop, she received a call telling her that her oldest son had been killed in an accident. She admitted that immense grief and sorrow overcame her. Even though she'd had an amazing preview into what happens when our physical bodies die, her heart still ached and longed for her son.

Experiencing grief and sorrow is a natural human response. It's how God created us. We see the emotions in Jesus when he wept at the tomb of His dear friend Lazarus.

When the mortal body of a loved one dies, our faith in the eternal life Jesus has for us does not disappear in our grieving. Well-meaning people might say, "Oh, but he's in a much better place now. He's healed and perfectly happy!" And while that is 100 percent true, it does not erase the pain of their absence. In other words, both feelings—joy at their homecoming and sorrow at their departure—can coexist.

One thing I hope to pass on to anyone who is going through, or will go through, a tragic loss is to remember that your faith has not disappeared or gotten weak if your grief and fear are great. Faith, grief, and fear can happen simultaneously. One does not cancel out the other.

I made the mistake of trying to push the grief and fear away and continue in my strength. I tried to use faith as my reason. If I had faith, I would know that God knows what He's doing, so I must dust myself off and keep going. This faulty reasoning kept me stuck. I had to let myself feel the grief and express my deep pain and sorrow to work through it and begin healing.

God wasn't judging me as a faithless, untrusting child. He was grieving with me. He felt my deep sadness and comforted and held me. I'm grateful to be loved by such a compassionate God who knows our weaknesses, continues to love us, and removes the guilt and shame we heap on ourselves.

David says it perfectly in Psalm 18:1-6, 19.

I will love thee, O LORD, my strength. The LORD is my rock, and my fortress, and my deliverer: my God, my strength, in whom I will trust; my buckler, and the horn of my salvation, and my high tower. I will call upon the LORD, who is worthy to be praised: so shall I be saved from mine enemies. The sorrows of death compassed me, and the floods of ungodly men made me afraid. The sorrows of hell compassed me about: the snares of death prevented me. In my distress I called upon the LORD, and cried unto my God: he heard my voice out of his temple, and my cry came before him, even into his ears. He brought me forth also into a large place; he delivered me, because he delighted in me.

Heavenly Father,
How grateful we are to be Your children! You are our high tower where we can run in and be safe. You created us with emotions;

they make us human and enable us to have compassion and love for others. The great grief we experience is proof of the great love we've known. We know that love comes from You, and we love You because You loved us first. Thank You for the great love with which You created and now lead us. Give us eyes to see others as You see them. Give us the ability to love others as You love them, and help us to always trust You, especially when we don't understand or agree with what is happening around us. Because Your will is perfect, we can be assured that whatever comes to pass will be perfect. We praise You and bless Your holy Name,

In Jesus Name,

Amen

Chapter 5

Prayer and Healing

*"I would rather teach one man to pray than
ten men to preach."*

Charles Spurgeon

My first experience with prayer was the one my grandmother taught me to say at bedtime:

Now I lay me down to sleep, I pray the Lord
my soul to keep, If I should die before I
wake, I pray the Lord my soul to take. God
bless my mom, dad, my sister, grandma ....

At church, I was taught to pray on the rosary. The only salutation I remember is:

> Hail Mary,
>
> Full of grace,
>
> The Lord is with thee.
>
> Blessed art thou among women
>
> and blessed is the fruit
>
> of thy womb, Jesus.
>
> Holy Mary,
>
> Mother of God,
>
> pray for us sinners,
>
> now and at the hour of our death.
>
> Amen

In catechism class, I learned the Lord's Prayer:

> Our Father,
>
> Who art in Heaven,
>
> Hallowed be thy name,
>
> Thy Kingdom come,
>
> Thy will be done in earth as it is in Heaven.
>
> Give us this day our daily bread,

And forgive us our trespasses,

As we forgive those who trespass against us,

And lead us not into temptation,

But deliver us from evil.

Amen

I'm amazed that I can still remember the devotions I learned at such a young age. Saying them more as a formality than as a conversation with God, I obediently did what was expected. I would mechanically recite the words and either go about my day or fall asleep. While I believed God heard me, I didn't anticipate an answer.

Later, as a teenager and young adult, my prayers transitioned into supplications for myself and those I loved. My understanding of God was that He was my Creator and Judge, a distant, all-powerful being Who watched over me but wasn't involved in my everyday life except to grant a request here and there.

I knew Jesus died on the cross for my sins, but I didn't understand that He was my Friend and Brother, someone Who loved me deeply and desired to have a relationship with me. I thought God expected me to be "good" by following the rules and living a moral life, and He would punish me for any disobedience now and in the life to come. I believed I had to say my prayers to stay in God's favor and obtain forgiveness from Him—until the day Jesus dramatically changed my life.

I was sitting in church, attending a ladies' Bible study, when I came face-to-face with Who Jesus is, what He did for me, and how much He loves me.

The program was part of a year-long study of Moses. Reading from the first five books of the Bible, we learned how God, through Moses, gave the law to His people, the Israelites. Leading up to my epiphany, I was listening to our speaker preach about the Tabernacle and how the priests were required to offer atonement for themselves and God's people through the blood sacrifice of animals. God had specific instructions regarding how and when the sacrifices would occur. The animals, for instance, had to be clean and unblemished.

I was absorbing a lot of information, some of which was hard to follow, but one point was clear: regular animal sacrifice was needed because people were sinning continuously.

With that grave picture of sin to highlight our deep need for atonement, God gave me a vision of Jesus, bloodied and beaten, hanging on the cross. For a moment, His form was as real and tangible as the person sitting next to me.

Growing up in a Catholic Church, I had seen many crucifixes and images of Jesus, so while the impression wasn't new for me, the spiritual mirage before my eyes created a shift in my soul that rocked my world. I suddenly grasped the depths of what Jesus did for me, the great sacrifice He made.

He suffered a brutal, painful death because of His great love for me! For *me*! And I saw how black my sin really was. I deserved death because of my sin, but Jesus took my place (Romans 6:23)! He died and took the punishment for me. I am forgiven and free because Jesus paid my debt with His blood.

I had always thought I was a decent person. I did my best to keep my nose clean and follow the rules. I could certainly point out other people who behaved worse than I had. But at this moment, I recognized how deep my sin ran and why it took an incredible sacrifice to pay a debt I could never pay. Romans 6:23 says, "For the wages of sin is death, but the gift of God is eternal life in Christ Jesus our Lord." A wage is something we deserve. If we work a job, then we are owed our wages. I deserved death, but Jesus gave me life! I fully grasped how He took all my sins onto Himself and suffered the punishment meant for me. He stood in my place. And He did it because of the great love He has for me.

Ultimately, I realized that Jesus' love for me was far more profound than I knew. The verses "all our righteousnesses are as filthy rags" and "For all have sinned, and come short of the glory of God" became crystal clear at that moment (Isaiah 64:6, Romans 3:23). I knew that any "good" in me wasn't enough and would never be enough. It was Jesus' sacrifice alone that saved me. Before He died, Jesus' last words were, "It is finished" (John 19:30). The Greek word for this phrase is tetelestai which means to bring to a close, to finish, or to complete. In Jesus' time tetelestai was commonly used in debt collecting to denote that a loan had been paid in full. It was also used in a judicial context in a court when a particular sentence was fully served. Finally, in a military context, this word was used to relay that a battle had been won. When Jesus hung on the cross and cried out "Tetelestai (It is finished)," he was declaring your debt of sin is fully paid, the judgment for your sin has been fully served, and the spiritual war against death, sin, and Satan has been completely won! IT IS FINISHED! HALLELUJAH!

For the first time, I saw Jesus as my Friend, Savior, and Husband. The Holy Spirit changed my heart that day. He opened my eyes to the truth of the Gospel I had heard my whole life but never fully understood. I left the church shaken and unsure of how to live with this new understanding and love that filled my heart, mind, and soul.

From the outside, my life didn't look that different. I was still attending church, homeschooling my kids, and leading a "decent" life. But inside, everything changed. I was no longer seeking to gain God's favor by following the rules and obeying His commands. I was doing these things because of my great love for Him and my immense gratitude for His love for me: same actions, different heart.

The most significant change was the time I spent alone with Him. I dedicated more time to prayer and reading His word. My prayers were different, too. I was more intentional about seeking Him and hearing from Him. It wasn't just about supplications. Sure, requests were still a part of it, but there was much more.

I learned that prayer is about acknowledging Him, praising Him, and seeking His will to be done in my life. It's about confession and asking for forgiveness for myself and those around me. It's about asking the Holy Spirit to guide, protect, and deliver us. It's about listening for His Voice and watching for His Kingdom to come. It's about connecting with a Holy God Who is near and cares intimately for me. No wonder prayer didn't have much power in my life as a child when I saw Him only as a distant, all-powerful being Who watched over me but wasn't involved in my life except to grant a request here and there!

Despite that life-changing epiphany, I would find myself, twelve years later, in a place that would test everything I'd learned.

Standing on the Rock

When Rob was admitted to the hospital, prayer was all I had. Although I hoped the doctors could help him, I knew, ultimately, that God was the One Who could and would heal him.

Tuesday, October 21, 2014, began like every other Tuesday in our house. The kids and I got up early, collected our supplies, and prepared to head off to Classical Conversations, our weekly community home-schooling day. I kissed Rob goodbye, and we left. A few hours later, I received a text from Rob: "I'm sorry to bother you. I know you're teaching, but can you please come home? I need you." I immediately knew something was very wrong. If he asked me to leave in the middle of class, something serious must be going on. He told me to bring our 15-year-old son, Brice, with me.

We arrived to find Rob sitting up in a chair with blood dripping from his face. Rob explained that he passed out as he got out of the shower. When he came to, he was lying on the floor with a cut on his face.

I immediately went into panic mode and started to call an ambulance. Rob stayed calm and assured me that everything would be okay. He didn't need an ambulance but wanted Brice and me to help him to his truck.

By the time we arrived at the emergency room, Rob was struggling to breathe. Fear was rising in me, but I tried my best to stay calm, not only for Rob but also for Brice. The nurses gave him oxygen, and he immediately started feeling better. We were relieved and patiently waited for a doctor.

After the examination, the doctor discovered two heart blockages: one was 70% blocked, and the other was 100% blocked. He must have seen the worry on our faces because he immediately said, "But it's okay because his heart has grown its own bypass. He has not had a heart attack, and his heart is pumping strong, just like it should be."

We were shocked! "His heart had grown its own bypass?" I asked. The cardiologist said that happened a lot.

"Then why is he having such a hard time breathing?" we asked.

"Shortness of breath is a symptom of heart blockages,"

the cardiologist explained. "We'll go in, do a double bypass surgery, and he'll be as good as new!" He further told us it was a routine surgery he had performed hundreds of times. We were relieved to have an answer and encouraged to know that a common procedure would correct his problem.

The doctor admitted Rob to the hospital and scheduled the surgery for first thing the next morning. That night, Rob asked me if I remembered the hymn, "Come, Ye Sinners, Poor, and Needy." Rob and I loved old hymns. He had been singing hymns his whole life, and I learned to love them, too, after I started attending church with him as a teenager. Although this one was familiar, I didn't remember it well. He explained that the song came to his mind as he was lying on the table in the emergency room just a few hours before. I was surprised since this wasn't one I remember him ever mentioning before.

He began to cry as he recited the verse that stuck out to him:

Come, ye weary, heavy laden,
Lost and ruined by the fall;
If you tarry till you're better,
You will never come at all.

His sudden show of emotion caught me off guard. The cardiologist had already been by to reassure us that this was a routine surgery; he had done hundreds in his career. The ultrasound technician had checked for blood clots and given the all-clear. Rob was generally an optimistic person, but he seemed to be unsure. I did my best to reassure him that all would be fine. I chalked up his sudden bout of fear as natural because he had never had surgery before. I had no way of knowing that this song was God's way of preparing Rob for what was to come.

The following day, Rob handed me his wallet, phone, and keys and kissed me as they wheeled him out for surgery. I retreated to the waiting room to pray and wait. This is where all our best-laid plans and hopes went up in smoke.

As soon as the anesthesia took effect, Rob's heart stopped! The doctors worked quickly to revive him and, upon further examination, learned the truth about Rob's condition. His shortness of breath in the days leading up to this incident was not because of heart blockages. It was because of blood clots in his lungs. We'll never know how they missed this in the emergency room. But now, we had a much bigger problem.

As I hit my knees in the prayer chapel, God reassured me with the verse from Jonah: "Salvation is of the Lord." Even though my world was spinning out of control, I could walk forward with courage, knowing that God was still in control.

After the first attempted surgery, my husband was transported to a second hospital that was better equipped to perform the extremely risky, difficult operation he needed. Only a handful of doctors in the country would even attempt the procedure. The surgeon who met me explained this, stating that two such specialists were at this hospital, and he was one of them.

Honest and direct, he said Rob may not make it out alive, yet with compassion in his voice, the surgeon assured me, "But, Mrs. Kiser, in that operating room, Robert will be the most important person in the world to me, and I will do everything I can to save him." I appreciated him for his honesty and kindness.

It turns out he was one of the best. Rob came through the surgery. The doctor removed all the blood clots from his lungs (there were so many!), and he repaired the heart blockages. It was just a matter of his lungs, heart, and blood healing. We were ecstatic and hopeful. Rob had come so far. In time, we would be walking out of the hospital.

To help with the pain and to assist in the healing process, the doctors kept Rob heavily sedated. Because of the drugs and the ventilator tube in his mouth, communicating wasn't easy. Every now and then, the nurses would lessen the sedatives to test Rob's brain activity, and we were encouraged to learn that there was no damage. He could motion with his head or hands to answer our questions.

During these times, I would talk to Rob about the kids and tell him how much we loved him. The boys visited some, but I decided seeing him in that condition would be too scary for the girls. They were so little. Instead, Rob's Uncle Billy suggested we make a video of each of the children to play for him. Rob loved it. He couldn't tell me, but I knew by the look in his eyes.

One day, when we were alone, I asked him if he wanted me to play a song. He nodded yes. I picked up my phone to pull one up and remembered the song he had mentioned, "Come, Ye Sinners, Poor and Needy," the night before surgery. I asked if he would like to hear the hymn. He nodded.

> Come, ye sinners, poor and needy,
> Weak and wounded, sick and sore,
> Jesus ready stands to save you,
> Full of pity, love, and pow'r.

Refrain

I will arise and go to Jesus;

He will embrace me in His arms.

In the arms of my dear Savior,

Oh, there are ten thousand charms.

Verse 2

Come, ye thirsty; come and welcome,

God's free bounty glorify,

True belief and true repentance,

Every grace that brings you nigh.

Verse 3

Come, ye weary, heavy laden,

Lost and ruined by the fall;

If you tarry till you're better,

You will never come at all.

Verse 4

Lo! The incarnate God ascended

Pleads the merit of His blood;

Venture on Him, venture wholly;

Let no other trust intrude. [6]

As the song played, I watched a tear roll down his face.

The words obviously meant a lot to him. I listened carefully as the refrain started to play: "I will arise and go to Jesus; He will embrace me in His arms." Wait! Did God give this song to Rob that day in the emergency room to prepare him to come to Him? I wanted him to stay with me. No! I did not want him to go to Jesus. I quickly turned off the song and found a different one to play.

I spent many hours praying in the ICU floor chapel. I'd find solace there when the doctors and nurses asked me to leave the room because Rob had suffered an episode and needed help. Sometimes, my sister would sit with me; sometimes, I went alone.

It wasn't just me praying. It was our church, community, and family; so many people were praying. Rob had numerous friends. He was an attorney, and many of his clients told me he was more like a friend to him than a professional advisor. They were praying, too.

The more people you have praying, the more likely God will answer your prayer how you want, right?

If that's not it, then what? The words you use? The person praying? Where you pray?

We were praying, praying with everything we had. People would message me with their prayers every day. Friends and family would pray with Rob. I prayed with Rob. I prayed for the hospital staff and the other patients on the floor. We prayed and prayed for 12 days, and then Rob went home. Now I knew. God *was* preparing Rob to arise and come to Him through that song, assuring him that Jesus was waiting with open arms.

He went to his forever home—to Heaven. His suffering was over, and he stood in the presence of the One Who created him. With his journey on earth complete, his life in eternity had begun.

So, what went wrong? Why didn't our prayers work? Didn't God hear us? Didn't God understand that, at 44, Rob was a young man with seven children to raise and clients to help in a successful law practice? He was a man of God who poured much of his time and energy into our church and community. Didn't He see that Rob was needed here because he still had work to do?

All the reasons why he should have survived seemed obvious to all who knew Rob, especially to me. Why didn't those reasons make sense to God? God let his body succumb to its injuries, and his heart ceased beating. Another man, Rob's age, was in ICU at the same time. His wife and I became friends. He was healed. She took her husband home.

Some may ask if our prayers even mattered. If God is sovereign and will do what He wants, what's the point of praying? Why does God heal some and not others?

All those questions ran through my mind then, and if I'm being honest, at other times when I've witnessed people going through circumstances that didn't seem to be changed or healed. You may have had the same questions. You would not be alone if you've ever asked these questions when confronted with unbearable challenges, possibly wondering if you even believe in God.

Can God Be Trusted?

Why don't our prayers always "work"? Why does God sometimes seem absent—as if He doesn't hear our prayers? Is God a King Who operates based on His changing emotions and feelings from day to day? Is He a genie ready to grant our wish if we ask the right way?

Here's the thing: God knows what we need even before we ask. He knows what we need before we even know what that is! He is omniscient. He knows everything from the beginning to the end. With His omniscience comes the fact that He knows better than we do. He has all the information. We do not. We may think circumstances are wrong or unjust, but we don't fully know a situation's intricacies.

Of course, it didn't make sense to me that a man as young and wonderful as my husband, with so much work left to do on earth, would die when he did. In time, I understood that God's thoughts are higher than mine, as expressed in Isaiah 55:8-9:

For my thoughts are not your thoughts,
neither are your ways my ways, saith the
LORD. For as the heavens are higher than
the earth, so are my ways higher than your
ways, and my thoughts than your thoughts.

God knows things I can't possibly know, which is comforting because if my thoughts were the same as God's, then either I would be God, or I would serve a God who was no smarter than me. Even if He decided to tell me why, I doubt I could safely carry that knowledge.

In her book *The Hiding Place*, Corrie Ten Bloom relates a story of asking her father about "sex sin," something she heard her classmates talking about.[7] Without answering her question, he pointed to a large suitcase and told Corrie to bring it to him. Obediently, the young girl attempted to pick it up. She struggled and pulled for a few minutes but could not lift the suitcase, let alone carry it!

Her father told her he would be a poor father to expect a small girl to carry such a heavy suitcase. Just like some objects were too heavy for her to carry at her young age, he explained, some knowledge would be too heavy for her to bear. He assured her that when she was older and better able to handle the information, she would find out what sex sin was. Corrie loved her father and fully trusted in his goodness and love for her, so she happily accepted this answer.

I fully trust in God's goodness and know His love for me is true and unchanging. When things are unclear and don't make sense, I remember that God's will is perfect. He can be trusted. As Martin Luther said, "This is true faith—a living confidence in the goodness of God."[8] If we genuinely believe that God is good, that He never changes and can always be trusted, then we can rest on how He answers our prayers, whether He says yes or no, and whether we know the reasons or not.

Why Do We Pray?

Why do we pray if God is omniscient and knows what we need before we ask?

God knows everything about us. He fearfully and wonderfully made us. He fashioned us together in our mothers' wombs (Psalm 139:14-15). He knows us intimately, from the workings of our cells and organs to the innermost secrets of our hearts. He knows our hearts better than we do! Yet, He still desires to hear from and communicate with us. He invites us into His sacred presence for our benefit. He desires a relationship with us. He created us for fellowship, and He loves us. He loves us so much that He sent His only Son to die so that we can come to Him and, eventually, live with Him in Heaven.

He also wants to conform us to His image. The more time we spend *with* Him, the more we become *like* Him.

Even though God knew exactly where Adam and

Eve were hiding and what they had done, He still interrogated them. He asked, "Where are you? Who told you that you were naked? What is this you have done?" God questioned Adam and Eve for their sake. He needed them to realize the seriousness of what they had done and to know their place in front of a Holy God. He needed them to confess to each other and Him because through confession, forgiveness and healing can begin.

For similar reasons, we continually encounter questions in our walk with God. He wants us to confess and acknowledge our sinful condition. He wants us to realize who we're listening to and what lies we believe. He wants us to grasp the seriousness of our disobedience and how it creates a separation from Him.

Confession is cleansing. "If we confess our sins, He is faithful and just to forgive us our sins, and to cleanse us from all unrighteousness" (1 John 1:9). When we try to hide our sins from others, and even ourselves, we end up far from God and unable to hear Him. As the Holy Spirit convicts, we are given the opportunity to confess our sins, which opens the door to let God reveal the lies we've believed from other voices competing for our attention.

Being honest about our emotions and sinful reactions is crucial to healthy relationships—with God and others—in every aspect of our lives. This open and honest communication with a Holy and Righteous God leaves us feeling encouraged and at peace. We can be assured that just as an earthly father loves and desires the best for us, our Heavenly Father wants the same for us more than we can comprehend.

How does this closeness and assurance come about?

Only through a regular and consistent prayer life.

Healing

As I'm sure you have witnessed, I have seen people healed and delivered after dedicated and consistent prayer. I've also heard accounts of people miraculously healed instantly after being prayed over. We see numerous accounts in Scripture of Jesus healing people with a touch, a word, or mud made with His spit and dirt (John 9: 1-7)! As a side note, I believe Jesus used his saliva, the dirt, and a pool of water to demonstrate His physical means of healing. At times, he uses medicine or procedures performed by doctors.

In another account, a centurion asked Jesus to heal his servant, who was sick of the palsy. Jesus agreed, but the Roman officer said, "Lord, I am not worthy that thou shouldest come under my roof: but speak the word only, and my servant shall be healed." Jesus marveled at this man's great faith and said, "Go thy way; and as thou hast believed, so be it done unto thee" (Matthew 8:5-13). The servant was healed immediately at Jesus' word.

In Luke 4:40, we're told that Jesus laid hands on the sick, and every one of them was healed of their specific disease. We also see Jesus healing people by casting out demons (Matthew 9:32-33).

Another time, Jesus healed a man at the pool of Bethesda. Scripture tells us that "a great multitude of impotent folk, of blind, halt, withered, waiting for the moving of the water" for their healing. Whenever an angel troubled the water, whoever jumped into the pool first would be healed of their affliction. One man, without a man to carry him, had been unable to reach the pool and remained impotent for thirty-eight years. Seeing him, Jesus said, "Rise, take up thy bed, and walk." The man was healed instantly (John 5:1-18).

Have you ever wondered about the other people lying around the pool? Why didn't Jesus heal all of them? Why just this one man? With countless individuals healed during Jesus' ministry, we can indeed surmise that many others who encountered Him were not cured or helped.

We know God heals. We see it in Scripture and our own lives. So, why did Jesus not heal everyone during His ministry? We can find a possible clue in Mark 2:17: "They that are whole have no need of the physician, but they that are sick: I came not to call the righteous, but sinners to repentance."

Jesus came to save His people, but not in the way they thought. The Jews were looking for a king to save them from the oppressive Roman Empire—a Savior to come and set up an earthly throne that would drive out the Romans. Instead of a military leader, however, Jesus came as a servant. Many were confused when Jesus told Peter to put up his sword (Matthew 26:52) and when He said, "Destroy this temple, and in three days I will raise it up" (John 2:19).

Jesus' primary purpose was to model how to serve and love one another and save our souls through the shedding of His blood. He came to fight and win a spiritual battle, not a physical one.

Yes, Jesus cared for the needs and hurts of many when He walked the earth, and He still does today. Nevertheless, sickness is a part of the cursed world we live in. It isn't until we get to Heaven that we will experience complete healing, where there will be no more pain and sorrow (Revelation 21:4).

I don't see anywhere in Scripture that promises every sickness will be healed. As a matter of fact, we read about sicknesses not being healed. In Matthew 10:1, we learn that Jesus "gave them (His apostles) power against unclean spirits, to cast them out, and to heal all manner of sickness and all manner of disease." This did not mean the apostles could indiscriminately heal anyone they wanted.

Matthew 17 relays the account of a devil-possessed boy that the disciples were unable to cure. The boy's father brought him to Jesus for healing. Jesus rebuked the devil, and the child was immediately cured. The disciples were confused. They asked Jesus why they were not able to do that. Jesus said, "Because of your unbelief: for verily I say unto you, If ye have faith as a grain of mustard seed, ye shall say unto this mountain, Remove hence to yonder place; and it shall remove; and nothing shall be impossible unto you. Howbeit this kind goeth not out but by prayer and fasting" (Matthew 17:20-21). The disciples could do only what the Holy Spirit enabled them to accomplish through faith.

Paul was an apostle who did great miracles and wonders. However, we see that Paul did not heal Trophimus at Miletus but left him there sick (2 Timothy 4:20). We also learn about Paul's helper Epaphroditus, who was sick to the point of death. Paul says that the Lord spared his life, but why didn't Paul heal him before he got that ill (Philippians 2:25-30)?

Man cannot manipulate God. God took him to the point of death for a reason. Scripture does not tell us why.

In 1 Timothy 5:23, Paul advised Timothy to use a little wine to deal with his frequent stomach issues and other ailments. Apparently, Timothy had an ongoing health condition that Paul did not attempt to heal; rather, he offered him practical remedies. Why did God not heal Timothy completely? Scripture doesn't tell us, but we can rest assured that his afflictions served a purpose.

Paul was healed from the bite of a poisonous viper (Acts 28: 4-5), yet he suffered "a thorn in the flesh" that was never healed (2 Corinthians 12:7). As we read on, we discover that God healed Paul of the snake bite to make His power known among these "barbarous people." We additionally learn that God allowed Paul to suffer his affliction of the thorn in the flesh to keep him from exalting himself above measure. Having prayed three times that it might depart from him, Paul reveals that Jesus said, "My grace is sufficient for thee: for my strength is made perfect in weakness" (2 Corinthians 12:9).

Rather than be depressed and anxious over this affliction, Paul says, "Most gladly therefore will I rather glory in my infirmities, that the power of Christ may rest upon me. Therefore I take pleasure in infirmities, in reproaches, in necessities, in persecutions, in distresses for Christ's sake: for when I am weak, then am I strong" (2 Corinthians 12:9-10).

Wow! Paul embraces suffering because it leaves space for Jesus to show His strength.

When we are empty, Jesus has room to work. When we have everything figured out and can operate in our own strength, we have no room for Jesus. If we want to experience God's power in our lives, we need to make room for Him by letting go of the idea that our circumstances should be perfect; otherwise, we're not being blessed. In truth, when our circumstances are imperfect, when we're suffering, God's abundant grace can be poured out.

Have you ever wondered what it would be like if everyone who prayed for healing received it? It seems to me that no one would die of a sickness or accident. How odd would it be to know that you would be healed through prayer no matter what happened to you? Would you still treat yourself right by caring for your health and avoiding unnecessary, dangerous risks? Would you still strive to be in a close relationship with Jesus?

What if I told you that—without exception—all who pray for healing will receive it?

There will be healing, but it is not always the type we might expect, such as relief from physical suffering. There will be healing of our hearts and minds and, eventually, eternal healing through physical death. We can rest confident in knowing these things.

Nothing is ever wasted with God. He uses all our pain and suffering for a grand purpose that He sometimes shares and sometimes doesn't.

I have strongly felt Jesus' presence in my deepest moments of sorrow and pain. It is when my needs are the greatest that I experience His most profound love and provision. Funny how that works: in my weakness, He is strong.

It's true. Don't misunderstand me. God always hears and honors the prayers of His children.

"Confess your faults one to another, and pray one for another, that ye may be healed. The effectual fervent prayer of a righteous man availeth much" (James 5:16).

Let us not automatically presume that this healing

will be physical. Also, let us not presume what the word *much* means: a great amount, but not *all*.

He doesn't always work how we want or expect Him to work. But we can be assured He is working. He is nearer than we think, and His goodness is greater than we will ever know on this side of Heaven.

Where does that leave us? Should we pray for others to be healed? *Of course!*

Should we wait with hopeful expectation to see God's answer? *Absolutely!*

Should we question God's faithfulness and goodness if we don't see the answer we were hoping for? *Absolutely not!*

God will do miraculous things through us and is faithful to hear us when we cry out to Him. Let us always be seeking His will and His ways through prayer.

Heavenly Father,
Thank you for shedding your blood for us.

Thank you for the gift of prayer. How wonderful to know that you are always with us and stand ready to hear us when we cry out to you. You are a good Father, gracious and kind. We trust you and rejoice that we can always run to you. We praise you in the good times, and we praise you in the difficult times. You give, and you take away. Blessed be your name forever!

In Jesus Name,

Amen

Chapter 6

Suffering

Rob began feeling short of breath about a week before we went to the emergency room. The symptoms would come and go. He had just started a new diet and decided that his body was simply adjusting. I was concerned, but Rob would reassure me, "It was just an episode; I feel fine now."

Months before this started, I began having strange feelings of dread—a sense of foreboding, nothing like I had ever experienced. I must admit, I used to be a pretty anxious person. Worry and fear came naturally to me, but this sense of unease was different and extremely strong. I had no reason to feel that way; nothing was out of the ordinary. I couldn't put my finger on anything I was afraid of. It wasn't something I could reason out logically; it was more like a sense or a feeling of something bad coming our way. I'd share my concerns with Rob, but he was just as stumped as I was. He would assure me everything was fine, and I would try to ignore the anxiety rising in me.

One day, I told him that my sense of impending disaster was growing stronger and that I thought we might be unable to continue living as we were; maybe we'd have to leave our home. I know it sounded irrational to him—it sounded irrational to me! But I couldn't shake how I felt.

After Rob passed, I was sitting in the waiting room on the ICU floor. Remembering the foreboding that had started the summer before, I realized that the sensation had lifted. The thing I had dreaded just happened.

During those months of foreboding, I was drawing closer to God and my family. I turned down social activities and spent more time alone with God. I now believe this was God's way of preparing my heart for what was coming. Job had a similar experience. After he lost everything, he said, "What I feared has come upon me; what I dreaded has happened to me" (Job 3:25). There's no way I could have known what was ahead, but God, in His grace, was getting me ready to face this trial.

Why Is There So Much Evil and Death?

I had the same questions many people face when something like this happens: Why was he having to suffer like this? Why did we have to suffer like this? They lead to the bigger questions: Why do we suffer if God is good and works all things for our good (Romans 8:28)? Why does God allow bad things to happen? Can any good come from suffering?

If God is our Sovereign Creator, unchanging, perfect in all His ways, and holy in all His works, then why does He allow so much evil to happen? Why doesn't

He stop it or prevent it? When the worst occurs, we might question His goodness or His power.

If we go back to the beginning, when He created the earth and everything in it, we find a God who created man and woman in His image. "So God created man in His own image, in the image of God created He him; male and female created He them" (Genesis 1:27). Since God has free will, He gave us free will, too. He didn't create robots He could program to act in a certain way. Love is not love if it is forced or programmed. God wanted us to choose to love Him freely, just as He chose and loved us.

You may have heard a friend say, "I wish my husband (or boyfriend) would surprise me with flowers (or romantic dates) more often." The obvious answer seems to be, "Tell him that's what you want." However, your friend might reply, "If I told him, he'd only be doing it because I pressured him."

We all want to be loved freely. None of us wants to be manipulated or forced to do something or be someone.

We don't want to be controlled. We like our free will, but it comes with a price—the ability to choose means we can choose well or poorly. Free will wouldn't exist if we could choose only to love and do good. Free will means we act according to our own discretion, which is different for everyone.

You may ask, "Why did God create us if He knew we would sin?" I heard this question while working on this book and immediately thought about how I felt when my husband and I were trying to have our first baby. The process took longer than we expected, and there were days when I wondered if we'd ever be blessed with children. We wanted a child to love and care for, a child who would love us. We wanted a family.

Were we anticipating a flawless child who would always make good choices and grant us a perfect and easy life? Of course not. We were willing to take the good and the bad to have this little human who would be part of Rob and me and make us a family.

I imagine God created us with the same desire. He wanted children He could love and who would love Him and live forever with Him. And, again, He wanted them to choose Him freely. If not given freely, it isn't love at all.

His first children—Adam and Eve—enjoyed a close relationship with God in the garden. They walked with Him and conversed with Him daily until they decided to eat from the one tree God told them to avoid: the tree of the knowledge of good and evil. "But of the tree of the knowledge of good and evil, thou shall not eat of it: for in the day that thou eatest thereof thou shalt surely die" (Genesis 2:17).

God knew that eating from this tree would open their eyes and their hearts to know evil, which would lead to spiritual death (separation from God) and, eventually, physical death. As a result of Adam and Eve's choice, from the moment we are born, we begin to die, and we are spiritually dead until we are born again through the Holy Spirit. Adam and Eve were created good and learned about sin after eating the forbidden fruit. We are born in sin, and after the new birth, we have the Holy Spirit to guide and teach us.

But God loved us so much that He already had a plan to redeem us! That plan would require Jesus to be born and live a perfect, sinless life, which would end with a painful death. Jesus would be the perfect Lamb, taking all our sins onto Himself and paying the price we could never pay. He would willingly go to the cross, and His blood would atone for every sin for all time. Through His obedience, we are made righteous and can enjoy fellowship with Him now and for all eternity.

God does not change as man does. Hebrews 13:8 says, "Jesus Christ the same yesterday, and today, and forever." Malachi 3:6 states, "For I am the LORD, I change not." God cannot deny Himself or change, so He will not take away this free will. Accordingly, people choose to sin every day. Can God intervene? Absolutely, and sometimes He does. When He doesn't, we remember His omniscient and omnipresent nature. Because He sees all and knows all, He has reasons for intervening or not intervening that we can't see. God can redeem the pain and work in circumstances that we could never begin to imagine would ever yield any good. His love is far greater and more profound than any love we've experienced with one another.

God does not cause evil. People can and do use their free will for evil.

Therefore, we must consider our nature as humans. Compared to the Divine, our righteousness equates to dirty rags; even our best intentions are often tainted with selfish motives. We further do not see what He sees, and our limited knowledge prevents us from fully understanding why things happen. No matter what happens, God is worthy of our trust.

He also loves to work through His people. This is where prayer comes in. God does not need us, but He desires to use us. "The horse is prepared for the day of battle, but safety is from the Lord" (Proverbs 21:31). He wants to hear from us, just as an earthly father wants to hear from his children. He delights in us and loves to bless us with good things. Our prayers are His delight (Proverbs 15:8).

The Results of Suffering

As I started writing this book, I was reading through the Book of John. I came across this verse: "Verily, verily, I say unto you. Except a corn of wheat fall into the ground and die, it abideth alone: but if it die, it bringeth forth much fruit" (John 12:24). The message got me thinking about suffering and how a seed must be buried in the dark, damp earth so it can die.

Think about that for just a second. The seed is doing fine by itself. As a matter of fact, if you keep a seed dry in a cool place, it will last for hundreds of years. Scientists have found grain in Egyptian tombs that can still be planted and will grow. Yet, for the seed to sprout, we must bury it below the soil where it is dark. Eventually, the original seed dies, but the tiny life inside grows when the hard outer shell breaks away. The new life pushes through the darkness to break through the earth, extending roots to anchor itself. The sprout stretches and grows toward the light, which it uses for direction and nourishment.

When we are at our lowest and darkest places in life, where our hearts break, new growth begins. Just as the seed's new life does not have an easy, straightforward path, we are similar. The darkness in our lives doesn't immediately disappear; instead, we must move forward to the light of Jesus. He does not let us walk through this darkness alone; He holds and walks with us.

Jesus promised, "I am the light of the world: he who followeth Me shall not walk in darkness, but shall have the light of life" (John 8:12). He illuminates our path (Psalm 119:105) and directs our steps (Psalm 37:23-24; Proverbs 16:9). And just as the plant uses the sunlight to create food for its continued growth, we use the Light of God's provision to sustain us and help us grow.

What a wonderful picture of the beautiful new life we

are given when broken and thrown into darkness! We go from being a tiny, hard seed to a beautiful, glorious flower or tree, free and thriving, growing taller and more robust in the light of Jesus. The vibrant new plant becomes fruitful, producing many other seeds and more life.

> "Think of the self that God has given as an acorn. It is a marvelous little thing, a perfect shape, perfectly designed for its purpose, perfectly functional. Think of the grand glory of an oak tree. His intention for us is "...the measure of the stature of the fulness of Christ." Many deaths must go into our reaching that measure, many letting goes. When you look at the oak tree, you don't feel that the "loss" of the acorn is a very great loss. The more you perceive God's purpose in your life, the less terrible will the losses seem."[9]

If we stay in the rigid confines of our hearts, relying only on ourselves and our abilities, we live *alone*. We live separate from God. We can only get so far alone; our strength and resources limit us. Such attributes, in fact, will run out at some point. We all face times of being broken and buried in darkness, but that's when we can begin the new growth process. Jesus will provide the nourishment we need to produce so much more than we ever could alone, and through the brokenness and suffering, we can find abundance.

> "If welcomed trustingly and peacefully, suffering makes us grow. It matures and trains us, purifies us, teaches us to love unselfishly, makes us poor in heart, humble, gentle, and compassionate toward our neighbor."[10]

The ultimate picture of suffering and dying to create new life is the one we see in Jesus. He was broken, rejected, and tortured. His brokenness resulted in the salvation of His children. Through the death of God's only Son, many lives were saved, and much fruit was produced. Jesus walked through great despair, gave up His life, and rose to the right hand of God, where He is forever glorified.

When we experience trials, we can be assured that we, too, can and will rise to the presence of our Father, whether on this side of Heaven or in eternal Heaven. God is so good to let us live in the light of the Holy Spirit's presence while we journey through this life.

The Bible teaches us that it is one thing to suffer for wrongdoing, but it is quite another to suffer when you've done nothing wrong. This is acceptable to God (1 Peter 2:20). This is what Jesus modeled for us. He had no sin yet suffered and died as a criminal. He went to the cross willingly, without bitterness, anger, or hatred. He even prayed that His tormentors would be forgiven (Luke 23:34).

Does this seem right to us? How could God send His only Son to such a horrible death? God allowed the suffering, and Jesus submitted to it to accomplish His purpose of salvation. Without taking on all our sins and suffering, along with the punishment we deserve, there would be no salvation. We would be separated from God forever.

Another result of His suffering is the trust it produced in us. We trust Jesus because we know He suffered in all the same ways we suffer (1 Peter 4:1). He is not a High Priest, unfamiliar with our challenges and pain because He was tempted in every way that we are but without sin (Hebrews 4:15). Jesus came to Earth and experienced every emotion as a human being. Therefore, He has compassion for us and understands all we go through. We are not ruled by an uncaring, distant God with no idea what it's like to live in this broken, fallen world. If no sparrow can fall to the ground without the knowledge of God, how much more is He acquainted with our pain and failures (Matthew 10:29-31)?

Would You Have Pulled Joseph from the Pit?

When we see someone suffering, we want to help. We

want to remove whatever is causing the pain or difficulty. This is a normal and natural response to our human condition. When bad things happen, therefore, we sometimes shake our fists at God and ask how He could allow it. We see only what's in front of us. We do not have the panoramic view that God possesses. If we could view everything He sees, we probably would not want to jump in and help. We would anticipate the good that will come from the suffering.

As parents, we have similar insights that influence our reactions. Observing our children ready to make bad decisions that will cause them hurt, we don't always sweep in to fix the situation. Knowing they will grow and learn from their mistakes; we give them room to mess up.

We cannot imagine the agony that Jesus' disciples and family experienced as they watched Him on the cross. They all would have taken Him down if they'd had the ability. While that would have been a relief in the moment, the results would've been disastrous! We would all be separated eternally from God and have no hope! This is why Isaiah says, "It pleased the LORD to bruise Him" (Isaiah 53:10). It did not please God to see His Son suffer. What pleased Him was what that suffering would produce.

> "Christ took suffering upon Himself and sanctified it. He changed it from an evil to a good. He took death upon Himself and removed the sting from it. Here was quite a new dispensation. Suffering and death still occupied an essential place in the general scheme of things, but they were not to be dreaded in the way that they were dreaded before."[11]

In Acts, Stephen endured a horrible death. Although we don't know much about him, we understand that he was "full of faith and power" and "did great wonders and miracles among the people" (Acts 6:8). As one of seven men chosen by the twelve disciples to help them serve the community of believers in Jerusalem, Stephen had to be "of honest report, full of the Holy Ghost and wisdom" (Acts 6:3).

Choosing the seven men was a great idea because "the word of God increased; and the number of disciples multiplied in Jerusalem greatly; and a great company of the priests were obedient to the faith" (Acts 6:7).

It's safe to say that Stephen did great work for God's Kingdom. However, the elders and scribes brought him in front of the Sanhedrin for questioning (Acts 7). Stephen gave an eloquent speech about God's historical dealings with Israel and Israel's history of rebellion against God. He accused them of rejecting Moses and the law and of killing Jesus, whom God sent for their salvation. His words did not go over well, and Stephen was stoned to death.

Can you imagine being one of Stephen's friends or family members witnessing his death? How could God let this happen to someone so faithful and devoted? Despite his strong faith and gift for preaching, Stephen was struck down in the prime of his life and ministry in a cruel and senseless way. At the time, I'm sure this made no sense to those who loved Stephen.

Stephen wasn't alone. Great persecution against the church existed at this time. All the suffering caused people to scatter and take the message of the Gospel "in Jerusalem, and in all Judaea, and in Samaria, and unto the uttermost part of the earth" (Acts 1:8). Before His ascension, Jesus told His apostles that they would take the Gospel to all those places. How did this happen? Through suffering and persecution!

What about Joseph, one of twelve sons born to Jacob? He and his brothers became the heads of the twelve tribes of Israel. Beforehand, however, being Jacob's favorite made Joseph's brothers jealous. They decided to kill Joseph. The oldest, Reuben, convinced the other brothers to throw him into a pit instead. He planned to return later and rescue Joseph. However, before Reuben could get back there, the brothers sold Joseph to the Midianites, who enslaved and imprisoned him over the next 13 years.

At the end of those 13 years, Joseph became a powerful leader in Egypt, second only to Pharoah himself.

Joseph ultimately saved Egypt and his family from a devastating famine.

Have you ever wondered what might have happened had Reuben returned in time to pull Joseph from the pit? Would *you* have pulled him from the pit to prevent all those years of suffering and despair?

We see the immediate, not the eternal. Our hearts are broken to witness the suffering around us, and it's natural to want to relieve or remove the pain. Nevertheless, while we see through a glass darkly, God sees clearly the entire picture from the beginning to the end. He has a bigger purpose than we can even begin to imagine.

"I Would Have Pulled Joseph Out" (2017) by Kimberly D. Henderson seems a fitting close to this chapter:

> I would have pulled Joseph out. Out of that
> pit. Out of that prison. Out of that pain. And
> I would have cheated nations out of the one
> God would use to deliver them from famine.

I would have pulled David out. Out of Saul's spear-throwing presence. Out of the caves he hid away in. Out of the pain of rejection. And I would have cheated Israel out of a God-hearted king.

I would have pulled Esther out. Out of being snatched from her only family. Out of being placed in a position she never asked for. Out of the path of a vicious, power-hungry foe. And I would have cheated a people out of the woman God would use to save their very lives.

And I would have pulled Jesus off. Off of the cross. Off of the road that led to suffering and pain. Off of the path that would mean nakedness and beatings, nails and thorns. And I would have cheated the entire world out of a Savior. Out of salvation. Out of an eternity filled with no more suffering and no more pain.

And oh friend. I want to pull you out. I want to change your path. I want to stop your pain. But right now I know I would be wrong. I would be out of line. I would be cheating you and cheating the world out of so much good. Because God knows. He knows the good this pain will produce.

He knows the beauty this hard will grow. He's watching over you and keeping you even in the midst of this. And He's promising you that you can trust Him. Even when it all feels like more than you can bear.

So instead of trying to pull you out, I'm lifting you up. I'm kneeling before the Father and I'm asking Him to give you strength. To give you hope. I'm asking Him to protect you and to move you when the time is right. I'm asking Him to help you stay prayerful and discerning. I'm asking Him how I can best love you and be a help to you. And I'm believing He's going to use your life in powerful and beautiful ways. Ways that will leave your heart grateful and humbly thankful for this road you've been on.[12]

Heavenly Father,
Thank you for suffering for us. Thank you for paying our debt and ransoming us from death. Thank you for salvation. Thank you for life and life eternal. Through your death, you have given us life, and through your life, you have shown us the beauty and goodness that suffering can produce. We know you see our pain when we go through difficulties and sorrows, and we are grateful for your comfort and tender care during those times. Lord, give us eyes to see the things you see. Give us hearts to love others as you love them. Remind us daily of your goodness so we will always remember how much we can trust you.

You are faithful and merciful and always
worthy of our trust. We love you.

In Jesus Name,

Amen

Chapter 7

How is This Good?

Whoever said that good would be easy? Does *good* convey "feeling" good or comfortable? What does *good* mean anyway? Isn't *good* subjective? What might be good to me may not be good to you.

Take food, for example. Olives are good. All kinds of olives. Black, green, kalamata, etc. I like to eat them with everything. Hallmark Christmas movies are good. Early mornings are good. You may think such things are good, too, or maybe you don't. So, if they are good to me but not to you, are they good? Who gets to define *good*?

A verse often shared with me after Rob passed was, "And we know that all things work together for good to them that love God, to them who are the called according to his purpose" (Romans 8:28). This was not easy to hear in the first weeks and months when the grief was intense and raw. If anything, the words minimized the devastation that I was feeling.

The Bible describes a married couple as "one flesh," so losing the other half of my flesh did not in any way seem good. I did consider that the verse was not saying that all things *are* good; it was saying that God works all things *for* good. There's a big difference! Even with that insight, I couldn't grasp how losing my husband, my love, and the father of my children could ever work out for good. Some things you can't see or understand when you have open wounds.

Still, what is good? Noah Webster gives over 40 definitions, such as "promotive of happiness; pleasant; agreeable; cheering; gratifying." We would label it as bad if something failed to produce these effects.

A second definition of good is "useful; valuable; having qualities or a tendency to produce a good effect."[13] This one reflects what I think when reading that God created the world and deemed it "good." As I said earlier, good is subjective. What may seem good to me may not be good to you. And what may be good to God may not seem good to us because He sees and understands things we do not.

We get another definition of good from Scripture. The rich young ruler came to Jesus and said, "Good Master, what good thing shall I do, that I may have eternal life" (Matthew 19:16)? Jesus answered his question with a question, "Why callest thou me good? There is none good but one, that is, God" (Matthew 19:17). From this exchange we learn that good can be defined by God's character.

Everything about Him is good; we also learn that none of us is good. Here, Jesus even claimed not to be good, but we know that Jesus is God. So, if God is good, then Jesus is also good. I think Jesus said this because the rich young ruler did not know that Jesus and God were one. Jesus wanted to point this man to the understanding that there is no goodness apart from God.

We do get glimpses of good in this life. "Every good gift and every perfect gift is from above, and cometh down from the Father of lights" (James 1:17). We also know that we live in a fallen world, marred by sin. Man's free will leads to sin and brokenness. Jesus even promised that we would have trouble in this world. However, He told us to be encouraged because He has overcome the world (John 16:33).

After reading Romans 8:28, I understand that "all things" refers to everything we will encounter in this life, every bad and good circumstance. Because God is good, He will work all those things for good. Again, remembering God's character as being the definition of good, the good He will work is to make us more like Him.

We know this from the next verse, "For whom He did foreknow, He also did predestinate to be conformed to the image of His Son, that He might be the firstborn among many brethren" (Romans 8:29). We were created in His image, and He uses the circumstances of this life to shape us more and more into the image of His Son. The good He works results in our looking more and more like Jesus.

For a long time, I believed that working all things for our good meant God would change my circumstances from bad to good—what I defined as good anyway. He would heal the disease, save a loved one from death, allow me to get the job I wanted, fix the problem, etc. When Rob passed away, I couldn't imagine how good would come of it because I knew Rob wasn't coming back, and the only way good could result was if I had my husband back and our kids had their dad. Again, the "good" I sought was wrapped up in my outward circumstances. This isn't what Romans 8:28 and 29 promise. Rather, the verses reveal that God will make us more and more like our Heavenly Father and Jesus. How incredibly good is that!

Circumstances are always changing. Whether life

seems good, bad, or downright horrible, the one constant is God. God is always good. We proudly proclaim God is good when great things happen. A healthy baby is born! The happy couple is married! The long-awaited answer comes! However, it's important to remember that God is still good when the baby dies, the couple breaks up, and the answer never comes. Through all the bad circumstances, God is always good. His goodness does not depend on what is happening to us. His goodness is static. And we can be assured that all those bad things do not happen in vain. God will use them to bring about good by refining us to look more like His Son, Jesus.

Changing My Circumstances

While walking through the painful first days, weeks, and years of widowhood, I just wanted it to end. I counted each day, thinking that the larger the numbers got, the further away from the pain of that awful day I'd be, and the better life would be. I could see nothing good about those days. However, the pain, confusion, and sorrow did not lessen as the number grew.

No matter how many days passed, my circumstances did not shift. I was still a widow and a single mom. I thought I could find good again if I could change my circumstances, so I set out on a new path.

When my husband passed away on November 2, 2014, I had been homeschooling our children for about 12 years. At the beginning of our homeschool journey, I knew being active in a community of other families was important. I needed encouragement and fellowship with other moms, and my children needed friends, too. We joined a local home school group and loved the opportunities to participate in field trips, park days, and other fun activities. A few years later, I discovered Classical Conversations, an organization that included these activities and offered a full curriculum taught by moms as they joined together in the community once a week.

I found a church that would host us and invited moms

to begin Loganville's first Classical Conversations community. As our program grew, I took on the responsibility of starting new communities in surrounding areas. In addition to homeschooling my children, I was now leading other moms and groups in their pursuits to educate their children. I loved it! Teaching was my passion, and I loved seeing other families thrive in their homeschool journeys.

After 12 years, everything about me seemed to change in this new identity of a widow. The interests I once had, including homeschooling, no longer appealed to me. Of course, I loved my children dearly, but I could no longer find the passion I once had for teaching and leading the Classical Conversations groups.

For the rest of 2014, we took a break from homeschooling since we were close to Thanksgiving and Christmas. We returned in January and, somehow, muddled through the rest of that school year. But as we began the next school year, I felt my heart moving further and further away, and I truly felt incapable of continuing our homeschool lifestyle. I decided to pursue a change. I thought if I just did something completely different and changed my circumstances, I could begin to heal. Circumstances would get better, joy would return, and life would be good again.

After many months of praying, I finally decided to start a business. Yes, I was leaping from teacher to business owner! This was no small undertaking. Two good friends joined me, and we purchased a Great Harvest Bread Company franchise. The kids started at a local Christian school, and my days became filled with building out a space and opening the bakery. For a few years, this was a great distraction, but I eventually realized that, although my circumstances had changed, my grief was still there. I was still struggling to find good and more unsure than ever of my purpose and identity.

At this point, I cried out to God for help, admitting that I could not continue in my own strength. I confessed how desperately I needed His direction and goodness. I surrendered to Him. I surrendered my idea that I could make everything good. I needed Him. This breaking down led to God's incredible mercy in picking me up and revealing His goodness.

He taught me that my joy and purpose would forever be unstable if I relied upon my circumstances. God was using the things in my current circumstance to make me more like Christ, which in turn allowed me to see the good, but I had to work through my grief to find it.

Becoming Like Jesus, Seeing the Good

Eight Reflections

1. Jesus, the Only Essential Part of my Life: Provider of Everything I Need.

Repeatedly, Jesus demonstrated His complete dependence and singular loyalty to His Father. He told His followers that He did nothing apart from God, and all that He did was given to Him to do by His Father. In John 8:28, Jesus said, "When ye have lifted up the Son of man, then shall ye know that I am He, and that

I do nothing of myself; but as my Father hath taught me, I speak these things." We see times throughout Jesus' life when He would break away regularly to be alone with God (Matthew 14:13, Mark 6:45-46, Luke 5:16, John 6:15, Mark 1:35). And, at His darkest hour, when the time came for Jesus to suffer and die, He sought God's presence in the garden of Gethsemane. Jesus knew all His strength and wisdom came from God. He relied on God to fill Him for the work He was sent to accomplish.

As of this writing, ten years have gone by since Rob arrived at his forever home. The grief and sorrow are still as strong today as they were back then. I miss him. However, a difference exists between the sorrow I felt then and feel now. Then, my sorrow was mixed with fear. Now, my sorrow is mixed with hope.

The fear is gone. God has cared for, provided for, and protected us. We have never gone without, neither spiritually nor physically. He has been the perfect Husband, Father, and Friend.

In the beginning, it was so hard to understand how God could take my husband away. Yes, *mine*. And my children's father. Yes, *theirs*. He belonged to us, and God took him. We needed him. All those fears arose because I knew how much we needed him; the future was unstable and scary without him. I remember thinking that it was unfair, even cruel, for God to take Rob away from us. I learned that all those fears and bitter, angry feelings were there because of my wrong thinking.

The truth is that Rob didn't belong to me or my children. He belongs to God. Without realizing it, I had made my family an idol. I looked to Rob and my children to provide everything I needed—physical provision, love, and identity. I was deriving my worth from being his wife and their mother. I saw my husband as an essential part of my life and couldn't understand how God could not see that.

The truth is that Jesus is the only essential part of my life. He is the One who provides everything I need. He is the One who desires and deserves all my worship. Yes, He gave me a beautiful gift in Rob. We had a wonderful marriage, and God blessed us with amazing children. When I look back on my life and consider it now, I realize that all the people in it—my friends and family—are all beautiful gifts from God to be loved. But none of them are responsible for my happiness or for giving me value. They are all blessings to be enjoyed and thankful for.

As I write this, Job's cry keeps coming back to me: "The Lord gives and the Lord takes away. Blessed be the name of the Lord" (Job 1:21)! I think Job understood this. He mourned and grieved over losing all the blessings in his life, but he knew that they didn't belong to him. They belonged to God, and He was perfectly right to give and take them away. Moreover, Job needed only God.

How freeing to have this revelation! Let God be God and remember where all my praise and worship is to be directed. I know the One I depend on for everything never changes and can provide above and beyond all that I can hope or imagine. I need His Spirit every day just to get up in the morning. I am nothing without Him. He has given me life, breath, and identity. He fills me daily with hope, joy, love, and strength. And so, like Christ, I understand the importance of staying connected to our Father, who provides our daily bread and living water (Matthew 6:11; John 4:10).

Not a human being on this earth can fill us like Jesus. Now that I understand this, loving my children and those around me is much easier. I'm not expecting them to complete or sustain me. Jesus, my Rock, has that job, and He does it perfectly! I'm free to love and serve them.

We burden our loved ones when we expect them to fill us in ways they never could. The weight of this expectation can be crushing for them, and often, it can cause them to retreat and distance themselves further from us, leaving us wondering why we can't connect with them.

We can appreciate God's gifts more deeply without relying on them to bring us joy. We can appreciate them, knowing that they are blessings that God has allowed in our lives but were never intended to validate or give us our identity.

When God created Adam, he proclaimed that being alone was not good for man. He created Eve to be his helper, not his God. When they desired to be like God, to know good and evil, they fell into guilt and shame. They hid and covered themselves. God created us for fellowship, but He commands that we worship Him and only Him. The first commandment says, "Thou shalt have no other gods before me" (Exodus 20:3). Looking to all our little gods to fulfill and sustain us makes us feel empty and lost.

All the people and material things in our lives are given to us to love and steward well. When we look to people and things for our value and as life's necessities, we cross over into idolatry. I still love my husband with all my heart. I love my children fiercely. I love my family and my friends. And I pray daily that God will help me see and love all people as He sees and loves them. But I know that none of them belongs to me. I don't belong to them. We all belong to our Lord and Savior, Jesus Christ.

C.S. Lewis said it perfectly: "If we find ourselves with a desire that nothing in this world can satisfy, the most probable explanation is that we were made for another world."[14] This is not our home. We are all made for another place. While on this earth, our primary purposes are to glorify God, love Him, and love others as we love ourselves (Mark 12:20-31, 1 Corinthians 6:19-20). I further believe that God, because of His great love and infinite mercy for us, will allow us to reunite one day in our forever home with Him in Heaven.

So, do I still think God was wrong for taking Rob home? No. He didn't belong to me. He belongs to God, and Rob has arrived at his destination—where I plan to arrive and where all my children, family, and friends intend to be. God created this place for us. Am I still sad that Rob's not here with me now? Of course. But I trust God and know He provides everything I need. He is the source of life and light.

2. "The Lord is My Shepherd. I Have Everything
   I Need" (Psalm 23:1-6).

Jesus demonstrated His trust that God would provide everything He needed. At the beginning of His
ministry, Jesus was led by the Spirit into the wilderness, where he fasted for 40 days and nights. Satan
took advantage of this opportunity and tried to tempt
Jesus. In Jesus' weak state of hunger, Satan tempted
Him with food. When that didn't work, he resorted
to tempting Jesus' pride by proving that He really
was God's Son. Finally, Satan tempted Jesus to take
on His God-given power and authority without going
to the cross. Of course, Jesus did not give in to any of
these temptations. He waited on God, knowing that
He would provide everything Jesus needed.

I've learned a greater sense of contentment and gratitude, knowing that God is the Good Shepherd Who
gives me all I need.

As a young mom and wife, I juggled many balls to
keep everyone happy. I thought that if I let one drop,

everything would bounce and fly out of control. I put many expectations on myself as if I were the universe's general manager! While under my own pressure, I created high expectations for my family.

High expectations can cloud our ability to enjoy what is before us and keep us constantly searching for what's not there, seeking the ideal that often doesn't exist. Keeping our expectations reasonable in the current social media era is more challenging than ever. The more we see, the more we want. And the more we want, the more we think what we have is not great.

Satan tried to tempt Jesus by showing Him what He was missing, potentially convincing Him that He needed something else. Satan is still doing that to us today. He tempts us with what we could have if only we'd compromise here or worship over there. He tricks us into thinking we can be the gods of our own world.

Losing the most precious person in my life shattered the world I had so carefully constructed and held together, or at least that's what I thought. Now

I understand that I just don't have that much power. Previously, however, sitting amid the ruins, I felt devastated and lost. Joy and peace were distant memories that would possibly never return.

This experience stripped me of any preconceived notions that I was in control and needed to have or achieve certain things to be content. I've since learned that contentment and gratitude are not dependent on people or material elements. Chasing the perfect job, experiences, or material possessions will not lead to fulfillment.

It's not about what I don't have and can achieve in the future; it's about what I have right now. It's about waking up every day, counting the blessings in my life, and remembering how grateful I am to be God's child. It's about being content in my current circumstances because I know the One Who is in control, and He can be trusted. Because I'm not constantly chasing more, I can slow down and enjoy the present and the beauty of the moment.

3. I Am Enough.

Jesus knew exactly Who He was and what His purpose was. When others questioned His claim to be the Messiah, He remained resolute and focused on His mission.

We might say, "Of course, He knew who He was! He was God in the flesh. God knows and sees all." While that is correct, Jesus was also a man. He was fully God and fully man. That can be hard to wrap our minds around, but it is true. The fact that He was fully man allowed Him to experience life as we experience it; this includes our every temptation and emotion. He walked through all of it perfectly, with no sin. He set an example for us to follow.

Of course, we cannot live perfectly as He did, but His example guides us. Seeing how Jesus walked boldly and confidently in His identity teaches us to walk the same way in our God-given identity. God has given each of us a unique personality and giftings. Unfortunately, we don't always understand the truth of this identity; we believe lies about who we are, or we may not like who we are and wish to be someone else. Through the tragedy of losing my husband, I've learned to love myself and be confident in the abilities and unique ways God created me.

For many years, I struggled with self-doubt and insecurity. I believed the lies other people said about me and the lies I constructed based on the trauma in my life. Both kinds led to the formation of a false identity that I felt the need to validate. I was constantly striving to prove my value and worth. I needed to prove to others that I was worthy of their acceptance and love. In many ways, I was striving to convince myself that I was worthy of love as well.

As I pressed into God, He began to chip away at the lies and unforgiveness that had become the foundation of my insecurity and anxiety. He revealed my true identity, the person He created me to be. He helped me see and love myself as He sees and loves me. Writing this book finally became possible because I grew free of the fear, self-doubt, and self-loathing that enslaved me for so long.

Michelangelo's quote perfectly illustrates the transformation that God did in me:

> The sculpture is already complete within
> the marble block before I start my work. It
> is already there, I just have to chisel away
> the superfluous material.[15]

As He chips away the stony parts, it can be painful and uncomfortable, but the process is necessary to reach the beauty within—a preexisting beauty of His image.

4. All People are Worthy of Respect and Love.

Jesus loved all people and deemed them worthy of respect and love. He often saw those overlooked or looked down on by others. One of my favorite examples is Zacchaeus.

Zacchaeus, a chief tax collector, was incredibly rich. Considered traitors because they were Jews working for the Romans, many tax collectors were dishonest, taking more money than what was owed to keep for themselves. The Jews resented paying taxes to the Romans and the people in charge of collecting the money.

Like many others, Zacchaeus heard that Jesus would pass through Jericho and desired to see the man who had done many miracles. A large crowd formed, and being a short man, Zacchaeus could not see over all the people. He ran ahead, climbed a sycamore tree, and waited for Jesus to pass.

Despite all the confusion as the crowds thronged Jesus, He looked up and spoke to Zacchaeus, calling him by name. "Zacchaeus, make haste, and come down; for today I must abide at thy house" (Luke 19:5). Those watching could not understand why Jesus would desire time with a sinner like Zacchaeus. After Zacchaeus' encounter with Jesus, he repented and vowed to restore all that he had stolen fourfold.

Jesus proclaimed that on this day, salvation had come

to this house. He had come to seek and save what was lost (Luke 19:1-10). Where everyone else looked at Zacchaeus as an unworthy, filthy sinner, Jesus saw him for who he was: a child of God who was worthy of love and kindness.

I've learned to see people differently. Everyone has stony places that must be chipped away. Everyone believes lies that keep them from walking in the authentic identity of who God created them to be. Everyone needs love, mercy, and grace. I have a deeper compassion for those suffering and a desire to lead them to the One Who can fill them, heal them, and guide them in the joy and purpose God created them for.

Consider the following excerpt from C.S. Lewis, The Weight of Glory:

> There are no ordinary people. You have never talked to a mere mortal. Nations, cultures, arts, civilizations - these are mortal, and their life is to ours as the life

of a gnat. But it is immortals whom we joke with, work with, marry, snub and exploit—immortal horrors or everlasting splendors. This does not mean that we are to be perpetually solemn. We must play. But our merriment must be of that kind (and it is, in fact, the merriest kind) which exists between people who have, from the outset, taken each other seriously—no flippancy, no superiority, no presumption.[16]

People are eternal. All of us have souls that will live on forever. Everything else in this world is temporary, fleeting. I've learned the importance of focusing on the eternal, not the temporal. We are God's workmanship, His delight, His beloved. We're to treat others as royalty, children of the King, because they are. Is this easy? No. We live in a fallen, broken world, and sin has marred everything, including us. But we have Jesus' example and can strive daily to live and love as He did.

5. Life is Short.

Jesus is eternal. He's always been and will always be. Yet, again, this is another concept that is hard to wrap our minds around. Jesus lived 33 years on this earth. His ministry lasted only three years. His life as a man was just a blip. He had a mission to accomplish, completed it perfectly, and returned to His place in Heaven. Our lives here on this earth are short, but our souls are eternal. Whether we get 33 or 100 years on this side of Heaven, compared to eternity, either amount of time is brief. Our lives with Christ in Heaven will far exceed our time here.

Like Jesus, we have a mission to accomplish. He has a purpose and plan for each of our lives. I now see life in terms of eternity, with this current home being a brief stop before entering into the presence of Jesus. This perspective gives me a greater appreciation for the brevity of life and the importance of living in the moment.

I used to worry a lot about the future, imagining what

might happen or what I would do if certain events came to pass. Losing Rob made me realize the control I carried on my shoulders was an illusion. Each day is a gift we unwrap every morning when we open our eyes! God is waiting to walk with us and guide us when we look to Him. We make our plans, but the Lord directs our steps (Proverbs 16:9).

Have you heard the saying, "The days are long, but the years are short?" The present can trick us into thinking we have enough time to do everything we want and live life to the fullest. As we grow, we realize how quickly the years pass and how short our time truly is.

After Rob died, I remembered that year's experiences: the fun summer we had traveling, the birthdays we celebrated, and Christmas and other holiday seasons we enjoyed. I considered everything we had done that year and planned to do in years to come. As we delighted in all these times, it never occurred to me to savor every moment because it would be the last. I assumed we'd have plenty more. Every moment—a birthday or a random game night at home—is much more precious to me now. I savor it and feel so grateful for it. Never again will I assume that tomorrow will come. Today is enough.

As Eleanor Roosevelt said, "Yesterday is history. Tomorrow is a mystery. Today is a gift. That's why we call it the present."

Tomorrow is not promised, so I've learned to live in the present. I am thankful for each day God allows me to wake up, and I look forward to the path He's laid out for me.

6. Whether Good or Bad, Present Circumstances are Temporary.

The Greek philosopher Heraclitus is credited with this saying: "The only constant in life is change." How true this is! We can count on people, places, and circumstances to constantly change. There is One, however, that never changes. Jesus Christ is the same yesterday, today, and forever (Hebrews 13:8). Knowing this comforts me as changes come. The Lord is my rock, fortress, strength, and deliverer, always and forever. I can trust in His consistent and steady nature (Psalm 18:2).

Welcoming our seventh child was one of the most joyous times in my life. Hannah joined four brothers, Josh, Brice, Russell, and Kevin, as well as two sisters, Rebecca and Leah. We were overwhelmingly thankful for the beautiful family God had given us. Life was full and good, with seven children, 13 years old and younger. I knew they would eventually grow up, but imagining a life without diapers, toys, and a house full of active, happy children was difficult.

However, just four short years later, I would find myself a widow and a single mom. At the darkest, most bitter time, I could not imagine how I would ever be joyful or full again. Life is funny that way. Our present circumstances tend to color our perception of the future. We get caught up in the immediate and lose sight of how the future could look. While I was surrounded by darkness and trouble, seeing any light was impossible. I could not imagine good returning.

When things are going well, we see only the good ahead and plan for good things to continue. On the flip side, we tend to see more challenges ahead with no way out when we're going through difficult times. It's important to remember that change is always coming. The good times will not last, and neither will the bad times.

We love the good times. Good times are easy and comfortable. We want to be happy and see our loved ones happy. But we also know that Jesus said, in this life, we will have trouble (John 16:33). Trouble is coming. We live in a broken world.

Nonetheless, each time we experience a trial, we are refined to be stronger and better equipped for the next trial. Every experience can grow us if we look to Jesus and ask Him what He is teaching us. I've learned to stop asking *why* and start asking *what*; what are you teaching me in this circumstance? We can walk away better, not bitter, to withstand future burdens and help others with theirs.

Life is a rollercoaster of ups and downs, highs and lows, and joys and sorrows; I wouldn't have it any other way.

7. Great Pain Leads to Divine Purpose

We call the day Jesus was tortured and killed *Good* Friday. I'm sure those closest to Jesus did not think there was anything good about that day. They were distraught and terrified. His disciples, mother, and friends were probably asking, "How could this be happening?" Jesus, their beloved master, was being treated horribly. The wrongdoing did not make sense. Sure, He had told them this time would come, but they didn't fully understand why or what it all meant.

They believed Jesus was the Messiah but thought He would save them from Rome and bring order back in a military sense. Instead, He was being hung like a common criminal! I'm sure if someone had gone up to Peter at that moment and said, "Don't worry, God works everything out for good to those that love the Lord," he would have cut their head off!

We now have the privilege of turning the page and can see what happened three days later. The chapter's ending tells us Jesus endured the torture to conquer death and save us. The good that came from His suffering couldn't come about any other way. Jesus was the only way. The spotless, perfect lamb. The only One to live a perfect, sinless life was the only One who could atone for our past, present, and future sins. Romans 5:19 says, "For as by one man's disobedience many were made sinners, so by the obedience of one shall many be made righteous." His suffering was necessary for our salvation. And that is good.

In times of hardship and suffering, we desperately want to feel better and get past the challenging circumstances to return to the place that felt good and easy. It's human nature to avoid what's hard and to seek what's comfortable. However, Peter tells us not to be shocked when suffering comes. He tells us to rejoice because of the glory this pain will reveal in us (1 Peter 4:13).

What we do with the suffering can make all the

difference between a half-lived and an abundant life. Rather than brand these times as "bad" and try to find a way to exit quickly, I've found that these bad times offer lessons that could not be learned any other way. Pain always brings us closer to God's divine purpose: to become more like His Son.

> And we know that all things work together for good to them that love God, to them who are the called according to his purpose. For whom he did foreknow, he also did predestinate to be conformed to the image of his Son, that he might be the firstborn among many brethren (Romans 8:28-29).

If God's "good" is to conform us to His image, then our suffering is working for this good by making us more and more like Him.

Suffering chips away the outer layer that looks to the world and our flesh for joy. Jesus knew where His peace and joy came from: His Father. He tells His disciples that if they know Him, they know the Father because Jesus perfectly reflects God. God wants us to reflect His Son. Suffering turns our eyes away from the kingdoms of this earthly world towards God's Kingdom. Suffering illuminates how imperfect and temporal the things are that we chase for happiness and glory. Suffering reveals the importance and perfectness of the eternal.

People become more precious to us, as does our walk with God; such matters are eternal. We begin to find good in our lives through loving and serving others, praising and serving God, and constantly communing with God through His Spirit, just like Jesus modeled when He walked the earth. We begin to enjoy a deeper appreciation for the gifts God has given to us without relying on them to bring us joy.

Good exists in all seasons of life, both joyful and sorrowful. I have seen good come out of this season of loss and pain. I've learned and grown in ways I don't think I could have had I not traveled down this road.

Would I trade who I've become and what I know now to go back? I wouldn't.

Do I wish there was an easier way to reach this place? Of course. Unfortunately, some places can only be arrived at by a particular path.

I've heard the following story many times, and while I don't know the original author, it perfectly illustrates that those painful processes lead to the most precious results:

> A group of women once studied the book of Malachi in the Old Testament. While reading chapter three, they came across verse three: "He will sit as a refiner and purifier of silver." They wondered what this meant about God's character and nature.
>
> One of the women offered to learn about the process of refining silver and report back to the group at their next Bible study. Without mentioning anything about her interest

beyond her curiosity about the process, she called a silversmith and made an appointment to watch him at work.

She later observed as he held a piece of silver over the fire and let it heat up. He explained that in refining silver, one needed to hold the metal in the middle of the fire where the flames were hottest to burn away all the impurities. The woman thought about God holding us in such a hot spot and reconsidered the verse: *He sits as a refiner and purifier of silver.* She asked the silversmith if it was true that he had to sit in front of the fire the whole time the silver was being refined.

The man answered, "Yes," and explained that he had to hold the silver and keep his eye on it the entire time it was in the fire. The silver would be damaged if left even a moment too long in the flames.

After a moment of silence, she asked the silversmith, "How do you know when the silver is fully refined?"

He smiled at her and answered, "Oh, that's easy—when I see my image in it."

Just like the silversmith holds the precious metal and watches it carefully the entire time it's in the fire, God holds and watches us. He knows our weak frame, so He carries us and remains closest to us as we walk through trials that feel like they are destroying us. But God knows we are not being destroyed; on the contrary, He knows the fire produces a beauty in us that couldn't be achieved any other way, getting us closer to His image.

8. Living with *The End* in Mind

As a 12-year-old boy, Jesus told His parents that He was going "about His Father's business" (Luke 2:49). Even at a young age, Jesus knew that His goal in life was to live for His Father and complete the work He had given Jesus to do. Every place Jesus went and everything He did was motivated by this singular objective. He knew His time was short, and He had His Father's work to accomplish. Jesus lived with *The End* in mind.

In the beloved classic *Alice in Wonderland*, the mysterious Cheshire Cat shares a poignant reminder of how important our end goal or destination is in life.

> "Would you tell me, please, which way I ought to go from here?"

> "That depends a good deal on where you want to get to," said the Cat.

> "I don't much care where—" said Alice.

> "Then it doesn't matter which way you go," said the Cat.

> "—so long as I get SOMEWHERE," Alice added as an explanation.

"Oh, you're sure to do that," said the Cat, "if you only walk long enough."[17]

Sure, we'll get somewhere as we move forward, but where will that be?

And how do we choose the right way to go when we don't know where we are supposed to end up? Daily decisions are painstakingly difficult, and indecisiveness and insecurity reign.

In contrast, knowing our destination is a beacon that guides us, giving us direction and purpose in life. If our goal is to become more like Christ, and we know our final resting place is Heaven, then that intention will affect how we live each day.

My life is different now because I know the battle is won! Jesus defeated death and sin. He adopted me into His family, and I am righteous in the blood He shed for me. Jesus did it all! Having the gift of His Spirit, I can enjoy a peace that surpasses all understanding, even in heartbreak and sorrow, because I know this current world is not all there is.

A time is coming when all the shadows will disappear, and we will see as we are seen (1 Corinthians 13:12). We will live in the perfect light of Heaven where there is no darkness. All our wonderful gifts here are just icing on the cake!

Is cake wonderful without the icing? Of course, but the earthly experience is undeniably sweeter with the icing. That's how I look at the eternal life that awaits us. It's perfect and wonderful and complete, yet God, in His goodness and grace, gives us so much more to enjoy while on our journey to that place.

God's blessings are to be enjoyed, not to last forever. This flesh will pass away, but our souls will go on to live in perfect joy and peace with God eternally (1 Peter 1:24-25). This perspective can greatly affect how we approach each day and circumstance.

Heavenly Father,

You are so good! You are perfect in all your ways and holy in all your works. Your goodness is beyond understanding! Thank you for sending Jesus to live a perfect, sinless life. Thank you for your Word, which teaches us what goodness means. Thank you for creating us in your image and using every experience to conform us more and more into that image. We would be lost without you. This world is not our home. Help us always to remember who we are and whose we are. We are your sons and daughters, perfectly created by you and for you. All glory and honor is to you now and always.

In Jesus name,

Amen

Chapter 8

Recognizing the Good

From the moment of creation, when God said, "Let there be light," good entered the world (Genesis 1:3). At the end of each day of creation, God saw everything He made and declared it good. Good is still here.

But let's be real: bad things happen, and they happen often. You've probably heard the saying: we are either coming out of a hard season, in a hard season or preparing to go into a hard season. That's the fallen world we live in; loved ones die, debilitating diagnoses are given, children go astray, and we experience financial ruin and traumatic accidents. We may be falsely accused of something or betrayed by people we love and trust.

Of course, none of us wants to go through heart-wrenching trials. Even Jesus cried out to God and sweated drops of blood, asking God to let this cup pass from Him as He prayed in the garden of Gethsemane before his crucifixion. Jesus knew His time had come to suffer and die, and the human part of Him was sorely grieved. We are made in His image. We grieve in these hard places, too.

Allow me to offer another perspective. What if we changed our thinking and considered such events and situations as training grounds for the people God created us to be?

Jacob's son, Joseph, is a wonderful example of someone who suffered through many dark years yet never forgot God or despaired. Although betrayed, deceived, and forgotten, he faithfully served others and maintained his integrity. Even in the lowest places as a servant and prisoner, he continually lived with a spirit of excellence.

God created Joseph to lead and save His people. We see Joseph being set apart from his brothers from an early age. Joseph, the youngest of 12 sons, found special favor with his father, Jacob. Of course, this angered his siblings. On top of that, God gave Joseph two specific dreams that showed Joseph ruling over his family. In one dream, Joseph sees himself binding sheaves of wheat in a field with his brothers, and their sheaves bow down to his sheave. In the other dream, Joseph sees the sun, moon, and stars bowing down to him. As Joseph shared his dreams with his family, their disdain for him grew. How prideful Joseph was to think they would ever bow down to him! Even Jacob rebuked his youngest son's arrogance and superior attitude. However, Jacob still wondered if the dreams had some significance (Genesis 37:11).

The brothers' envy drove them to devise a plan to kill Joseph, "the dreamer" (Genesis 37:18-19). However, the oldest brother, Reuben, suggested they cast him into a pit instead with the intention of rescuing him later. Then, upon seeing merchantmen traveling to Egypt, Judah recommends they sell him as a slave. "Judah" means praise. Consider that "praise" is what lifted Joseph from the pit. When we're in despair and feel like we are in a pit too deep to escape, we can turn to praise to lift us out.

The brothers then took the special coat Jacob made for Joseph, ripped it to shreds, covered it in animal blood, and presented it to their father. Jacob grieved mightily when he believed his son was dead.

The merchantmen took Joseph to Egypt and sold him to Potiphar, an officer of Pharoah. After this account, the Bible says, "And the LORD was with Joseph, and he was a prosperous man; and he was in the house of his master the Egyptian" (Genesis 39:2).

When I learned this story, I had to make sure I understood it correctly. Joseph was betrayed by his brothers and sold into slavery, yet the LORD was with him, and Joseph was prosperous. If I heard a story today of a 17-year-old boy thrown away by his family and sold into slavery, I would not think God was with him or that he was in any way prosperous. This tells me that no matter what is happening, we can be assured that God is with us and will lead and bless us—only maybe not in the ways we think He should. We can be certain, however, that His nature is never to leave us and always to help us succeed wherever we are and in whatever circumstance.

Quite evidently, God was with Joseph, who quickly became Potiphar's right-hand man and oversaw his entire house. Joseph took his job seriously and understood that Potiphar had given him complete control over all his affairs. When Potiphar's wife throws herself at Joseph and asks him to sleep with her, Joseph tells her that he cannot do such a wicked thing to his master or sin against God in this way; he tells her that Potiphar trusts him, and he will never do anything to break that trust. Potiphar trusted Joseph so much that he didn't even concern himself with the details of the everyday affairs in his house (Genesis 39:6).

Out of her anger at being refused, she falsely accused Joseph of attacking her. Potiphar believed his wife's claims and, in a rage, threw Joseph in prison.

Again, we read, "But the LORD was with Joseph, and showed him mercy, and gave him favor in the sight of the keeper of the prison" (Genesis 39:21). To the outsider, it seems that God has once again deserted Joseph. In our limited view, a good man is falsely accused and punished. Skipping ahead to the ending of his story, we know that this circumstance is leading Joseph to his purpose and to the good that God is working.

Even here, Joseph served and behaved with the same integrity and excellence that he did in Potiphar's house. Like Potiphar, the prison keeper left everything under Joseph's care and was unconcerned with details. He implicitly trusted Joseph. Here again, we see the word prosper. "...the LORD was with him, and that which he did, the LORD made it to prosper" (Genesis 39:23). In a prison! Yes, even in a prison, Joseph prospered.

This is a lesson for us. No matter our circumstances or situation, we will prosper if the Lord is with us. Joseph exemplifies the importance of staying true and faithful to the responsibilities before us and serving with integrity no matter where we are.

Do you feel like the Lord is with you? What might Joseph have felt? Scripture doesn't give us details, but I imagine that his father, Jacob, shared the stories about God he had heard from his grandfather and father, Abraham and Isaac, respectively. Joseph believed that the God who blessed and led his forefathers was the same God who led him. And the same God who kept his promises with them would do the same with Joseph.

We know God spoke to Joseph in those early dreams because, in Genesis 42, we read that his brothers eventually bow down to him. Did Joseph know his dreams were from God so many years before? I believe so, and

I think he trusted God to fulfill all His promises. How else could he have endured so many years of suffering and trials with an attitude of strength and excellence in the presence of his human masters?

In the next part of Joseph's story, we see Joseph's connection to God in the interpretations God gave him of his fellow prisoners' dreams. Most importantly, we see the Spirit of God dwelling within him.

After some time, the king of Egypt, angry with his butler and baker, sent them to Joseph's prison. Joseph was put in charge of them. Genesis 40:4 says, "...they continued a season in ward." I'm not sure how long this continued, but enough time passed for Joseph to form a relationship with them.

One morning, Joseph noticed they were sad. (I love this part of the story, which depicts how Joseph loved his fellow prisoners.) Being the man in charge, he could have pushed them around but instead developed a relationship with them and was sensitive to their feelings. We sometimes find it hard to care when others are hurting if we are nursing our hurts. Despite his persecution, however, love and compassion flowed from Joseph, and he desired to help them.

When Joseph asked them why they were sad, they said they had dreams on the same night and did not know what they meant. Joseph replied, "Interpretations belong to God. Tell me the dreams" (Genesis 40:8).

After hearing their dreams, Joseph told the butler his dream meant that Pharaoh would release him from prison in three days and reinstate him at the palace. Unfortunately, Pharaoh would hang the baker on a tree, and the birds would eat his flesh. Both interpretations came to pass. (I love how Joseph was quick to tell them that the interpretations were from God.)

Yet again, Joseph faced disappointment. He had hoped that once the butler returned to the palace, he would tell Pharaoh how Joseph was stolen from his home, wrongly accused, and imprisoned. The butler, however, forgot about Joseph and never mentioned him (Genesis 40:14-15, 23).

How many of us would give up at this point and say, "God doesn't see me. He doesn't care. I'm going to be stuck in this prison for the rest of my life!" I can certainly see myself despairing if I were at this point in Joseph's life.

As a young boy, God gave him two dreams of being a great ruler, with others bowing down to him, yet here he was, a prisoner. No one knew the truth about who he was, and it seemed no one would. How could they? He was in a dungeon, locked away and forgotten. When we face hopeless situations and cannot see past the darkness, let's remember that God has not forgotten us. He does see us, and He is working out His perfect will.

Two more years passed, and then something incredible happened that forever changed Joseph's life. Pharaoh, King of Egypt, had two troublesome dreams in one night. He sent for his magicians and wise men to interpret their meaning, but no one could (Genesis 41:1-8). Finally, after two years, the butler remembered Joseph and told Pharaoh about his fellow prisoner who had correctly interpreted his and the baker's dreams.

After being imprisoned for over three years, Joseph had to shave his beard and change his clothes to make himself presentable when Pharaoh summoned him (Genesis 41:14). He was now 30 years old, approximately 13 years after his brothers sold him. Upon meeting Joseph, Pharaoh shared that he heard Joseph could interpret dreams. Again, Joseph was quick to correct Pharaoh, saying, "It is not in me: God shall give Pharaoh an answer of peace" (Genesis 41:16).

Joseph revealed that God sent the dreams to warn Pharoah about the future. After seven years of plenty throughout Egypt, seven years of famine would follow. The famine would be so great that the seven years of plenty would not be remembered. Joseph disclosed that God had given him two dreams so Pharoah would know that the message was from God and that the events would soon unfold. Joseph then told Pharoah he needed to appoint a wise man who could organize officers to take up the fifth part of the grain grown during the seven years of plenty and store it in preparation for the famine.

Amazed by Joseph's wisdom, Pharoah immediately recognized that Joseph had the Spirit of God in him (Genesis 41:38). Unable to think of a better person, Pharoah made Joseph second only to himself. He removed his ring, put it on Joseph's hand, dressed him in fine linen, and secured a gold chain around his neck. After 13 years of being mistreated and unseen, Joseph was among the most important men in Egypt, second only to Pharoah.

For the third time, Joseph was put in a leadership position—first, another man's house, then a prison, and now a nation. Each man who'd entrusted him could rest knowing that Joseph had everything in hand and would do an excellent job.

Jesus said, "He that is faithful in that which is least is faithful also in much" (Luke 16:10). In the parable of the talents, Jesus commended his faithful servants and rewarded them by making them rulers over many things because of their faithfulness in few things. He invited them into the joy of the Lord! (Please read Matthew 25:14-30.) Joseph proved his faithfulness by first serving his father, and over time, God increased his responsibilities and influence as he proved faithful in each one.

What kept Joseph going through those years of suffering and uncertainty? The Spirit of God resided in Joseph. Even Pharoah recognized it. With Joseph's suggestion to find a wise and discreet man to prepare Egypt for the famine, Pharaoh proclaimed, "Who could be wiser and more discreet than someone with the Spirit of God" (Genesis 41:38)? How amazing is that! We don't think of Pharoah as a follower of God, yet he still recognized God's Spirit in Joseph.

How did Joseph acquire this Spirit of God? In the Bible, we're not introduced to the Holy Spirit until Jesus nears the end of His ministry. He tells His disciples that after He leaves, He will send the Comforter to them, Who is the Spirit of truth. This Spirit will guide them into all truth and show them things to come

(John 15:26, 16:13). Joseph lived hundreds of years before Jesus, so how he had God's Spirit is a mystery.

We know God is part of the trinity: Father, Son, and Holy Spirit. In Genesis 1:26, God said, "Let us make man in *our* image, after our likeness." He doesn't say after my image but after our image. Jesus and the Holy Spirit were present at the very beginning of Creation. God is the Holy Spirit, and He is Jesus. They're three in one. It makes sense that if we see God in Joseph's life, we'd also see the Holy Spirit.

The same Spirit that guided and sustained Joseph lives in us.

How can we access the fruit of the Spirit? "I am the vine, ye are the branches: He that abideth in me, and I in him, the same bringeth forth much fruit: for without me ye can do nothing" (John 15:5). That's it! Abiding in God. While abiding in Him, we have access to every good gift: love, joy, peace, longsuffering, gentleness, goodness, faith, meekness, and temperance.

The fruit of the Spirit encompasses the good we can always access. It's easy to view all of life through the lens of the flesh, but Romans reminds us that a carnal mindset leads to death (Romans 8:6). The carnal mind focuses on the things of this world, temporal things. Hardships and difficulties are part of this life, so trying to order and arrange our present circumstances with the expectation of finding joy will always lead to disappointment. We live in a fallen and broken world, and continually giving our attention to what our eyes can see will result in anxiousness and depression.

Our thoughts become our actions, which then become who we are. The same passage says being spiritually minded leads to life and peace (Romans 8:6). As born-again Christians, we have the Spirit of God dwelling within us. Spiritually minded thoughts become our actions, which then become who we are.

How often do you take a moment to consider your thoughts? To see the good (because it's always there), remember that your thoughts need to dwell on spiritual things and the One who is the source of everything perfect and good. The more time you spend with God, the more sensitive you will become to hearing the Spirit as He guides you into all truth. This mindset opens your eyes to the good around you and to the good that is coming.

Each situation prepared Joseph for his divine assignment. God was always near and bestowed favor on him. While hard to imagine God is beside us when we are hurting, we can be confident that He is. We might see our circumstances as hopeless, but that doesn't mean God isn't working. Just the opposite. He is using the time to sharpen us and prepare us for the greater call He has for us. First and foremost, the call to become like His Son, Jesus. And he's allowing circumstances to shape and refine us for the work He wants us to do.

"For we are his workmanship, created in Christ Jesus unto good works, which God hath before ordained that we should walk in them" (Ephesians 2:10). God ordained that Joseph would save many people from famine. What kind of ruler would Joseph have been if he had gone directly from his father's house to Pharaoh's? We don't know, but I'm certain the 13 years between the two were productive training for him.

What good works has God ordained for you? You may not know the answer to that right now, but you can trust that the place He has you in this very moment is your training for that work. You can also trust that He is a good Father, ready to comfort and lead you.

Are you confused about something? Ask Him for clarity.

Are you having doubts? Ask Him for assurance.

Are you disappointed? Ask Him for hope.

Are you sad? Ask Him for joy.

Stay in close fellowship with Him. Pour out your heart to Him and ask Him all your questions. Ask Him to speak to you and guide you. Praise Him. Thank Him for all his benefits. Then, wait for His timing. He hears you.

Joseph waited 13 years but never gave up or wallowed in self-pity. He served to the best of his ability, and God ultimately brought healing and restoration through a redeemed relationship with his father and brothers. God gave him children and grandchildren. Ephraim's children of the third generation and Manasseh's children were "brought up upon Joseph's knees" (Genesis 50:23). He died at the ripe old age of 110.

I'm sure Joseph had his moments of weariness and doubt. He was human, just like us. Rather than let those moments define and rule over him, he looked to God for strength. More than that, he believed in God's promises.

We serve the same God. He has not changed. Will any of us be called to rule over a nation? Maybe, maybe not. No matter the work God has called us to do, we can be assured that it is perfect, good, and important. God doesn't do anything halfway, and just as He is perfect, His will is perfect.

I am honored and humbled to know He created me

with a special purpose and identity—one that is different from anyone else He's created. He has created you, my friend, with a unique purpose and identity. Why? Because He wanted you in His kingdom! You! Me! Wow! That thought is overwhelmingly wonderous.

It's hard to wrap my mind around the millions of people He's created uniquely and how He longed for and wanted each of us. A snowflake is often the example used, and it gets me a little closer to that realization. When I'm watching snow from a window, I see similar dots of white, all falling and collecting into a white blanket. If observed under a microscope, the intricate differences that make each distinctive appear, and, amazingly, no two snowflakes are alike!

We may resemble each other and have similar personalities, goals, and jobs. However, God created each of our hearts and DNA in a remarkable way, unlike any other person. I am not the only woman to experience widowhood, but the details of my experiences and the way God created my heart and mind are uniquely different. The same is true for all of us. We are all fearfully and wonderfully made, fashioned together by God's Hand in our mother's womb (Psalm 139:14-15).

I don't know what season you are in right now. It may be difficult, even impossible, to see any good. I understand. I've been there, too. But let me encourage you. God is very, very close. He loves you with a perfect love (1 John 4:18). He created you in His image to reflect His nature (Genesis 1:27). He is refining you for His purpose (Ephesians 2:10). The same Spirit that rose Jesus from the grave is living inside you (Romans 8:11). Abide in Him, and He will abide in you (John 15:4). Draw everything you need from Him. He is the vine, and you and I are the branches. We can do nothing apart from Him (John 15:5). You are not alone. Your Heavenly Father has everything you need and stands ready to fill you.

> Heavenly Father,
> We marvel at your perfect will and are so thankful to be loved by you, the one and only true and living God. Thank you for creating each one of us in such a unique and

beautiful way and for reminding us of your presence in a world that is often evil and dark. We know you have good plans for us. We will be encouraged in both the joyous places and the devastating ones because we know you have good plans for us. You are our strong tower; we can run to you and be safe. What a joy it is to be able to focus our eyes and hearts on you to lead us! There is no one like you, Father. There is no name greater than Your Name. Help us to remember to live and work as to the Lord and not to men, knowing that your perfect will is being accomplished. We love you and praise you. Holy, holy, holy is the Lord Almighty! The whole earth is full of your glory.

In Jesus Name,

Amen

Chapter 9

A Reluctant Widow

I was in the room when my husband passed from his physical body and entered Heaven. I felt his hand grow cold. I watched as they unhooked all the machines, and everything went quiet. I saw the shell of my once happy, vibrant husband in the casket at the funeral home and watched as they lowered him into the ground. Yet, it didn't seem real.

I'd find myself listening for the garage door to open every night. I'd lay in bed waiting for him to enter our bedroom. I hated this new life. I didn't want to be a widow. I didn't want to be a single mom. As a matter of fact, I refused to be these things! This wasn't supposed to be my life. I had decreed as a child that I would never be a single mom and have my kids grow up without a father. My father left our family when I was very young, and I did not want that for my children.

About six months after Rob passed, I got in the van one morning, started it up, and saw the check engine light shining brightly. I immediately collapsed into tears! I stared at the light and admitted the truth: "I am a single mom. I am a widow."

You see, taking care of the vehicles was Rob's job. I just drove it. But now, this light was something that needed my attention. It was now my responsibility. This was the moment I stopped denying the obvious, which was a massive breakthrough for me. I spent so much time and energy denying and pushing away who I was and where I was, which just heaped more and more grief and disappointment in my life. I couldn't bring my husband back, so fighting against it only kept me spinning in a self-defeating cycle.

It reminds me of when Jesus asked Paul, "Why do you kick against the pricks" (Acts 26:14)? A farmer would jab an ox with a prick to coax it in the direction it needed to go. Oxen are stubborn. They kick at the prick. Eventually, they learn it's less painful to go in the direction of the prick than to "kick against it." They realize it's futile to resist the farmer's will. I was kicking against the pricks for months. I did not want to accept this new life and God's will. When I finally submitted, surrendered, and started walking in the reality of my new life, dealing with challenges became a little easier every day.

Submitting to this new life was hard. I did not feel equipped for the calling of a widow. I was just one person now taking on the role of two people. Have you ever heard the saying, "God won't give you more than you can handle?" I don't know where this saying began, but it is a lie! The world constantly gives us more than we can handle, reminding us of our shortcomings and our constant need for God's help and strength.

Has there ever been a time when you felt inadequate or ill-prepared for a task or even the season of life you were in? You're not alone! I can safely say that we've all been there. Although such times are difficult and uncomfortable, they remind us of our need for Jesus. They help us turn our focus from ourselves to our Savior.

God is good to include testimonies in Scripture of people, just like us, who were asked to do big things for Him yet questioned their abilities. In the book of Judges, Gideon was one of them.

Judges details a time in Israel's history when God's people turned from Him and followed the fake gods of the people living around them. There were no kings to lead them. God was their king, but they did not obey or live for Him. Angered, God allowed their enemies to oppress them. Nevertheless, our faithful and loving God heard their cries for help and sent a judge to deliver them. Once they were delivered and experienced peace again, they slowly turned away from God and fell back on worshipping and serving fake gods, like Baal and Ashtaroth. Again, God allowed their enemies to oppress them, and the cycle repeated over and over.

Gideon

One of the judges God sent to deliver His people was Gideon. And where was Gideon when the Lord called Him? He was hiding in a winepress! Gideon feared his people's enemies, the Midianites, so he was threshing wheat in a winepress to stay safe from them. Yep, the hero of this story, the one God chose to deliver His people from the great Midianites, was hiding. Doesn't sound much like hero material to me! However, this is just the kind of person God chooses to work through.

> "For ye see our calling, brethren, how that not many wise men after the flesh, not many mighty, not many noble, are called: But God hath chosen the foolish things of the world to confound the wise; and God hath chosen the weak things of the world

to confound the things which are mighty"
(1 Corinthians 1:26-27).

Why is that? Why does God choose the weak ones to bring His will to pass?

"And base things of the world, and things which are despised, hath God chosen, yea, and things which are not, to bring to nought things that are: *That no flesh should glory in His presence.* But of Him are ye in Christ Jesus, who of God is made unto us wisdom, and righteousness, and sanctification, and redemption: That, according as it is written, He that glorieth, let him glory in the Lord" (1 Corinthians 1:28-31).

God knows how easy it is for us to get puffed up and proud. He wants us to remember that no good thing in us brings about victories in our lives. God gets the glory for it all!

As Gideon was working in this winepress, an angel suddenly appeared and said, "The LORD is with thee, thou mighty man of valour" (Judges 6:12). I don't know about you, but if an angel suddenly appeared from out of nowhere, I don't think my first response would be to contradict him. Nonetheless, that is exactly what Gideon did! To paraphrase, Gideon said, "Oh, really! The LORD is with us? If the LORD is with us, why are we in this mess with the Midianites? Where are all the miracles our fathers and grandfathers told us about that God did when He saved them from Egypt? The LORD is not with us. He has forsaken us into the hands of the Midianites" (Judges 6:13).

Although I wouldn't have expressed such thoughts out loud, I can sympathize with Gideon. When we're walking through dark and difficult circumstances, it often feels like God is not there. We assume He has left us because He isn't doing anything about our struggle. Grief and fear cloud our perception and cause us to forget the truth of Who God is. We forget the character of God, that He never changes and never forsakes us. He loves us so much that He gave His only Son so that we would have eternal life (John 3:16). God would never leave us and is always near. God loves us, and

His compassion and mercies are new every morning (Lamentations 3:22-23).

It's interesting to note the title the angel gave to Gideon: "Mighty man of valor." From our outside perspective, Gideon does not seem courageous as he hides from his enemies and clearly wasn't feeling very brave if he was hiding. This is something else that happens when we go through a traumatic event or season; not only do we forget the character of God, but we also forget who we are.

Our fear opens the door for Satan, the enemy of our souls. He is continually walking about seeking whom he may devour (1 Peter 5:8). When we are anxious and fearful, we open the door to his attack. He loves to tell us lies about God and ourselves. In our weak state, we believe these lies and forget the truth of Who God is and who we are. God called Gideon a mighty man of valor because that is who he was. Gideon believed the opposite because his fear allowed Satan an opening into his mind. An angel of God had to remind Gideon of the truth: God is with you, and you *are* a mighty man of valor!

We need these reminders, too! Instead of letting fear grip us and allowing Satan to mislead us, we need to be reminded of the truth. We can go to God's Word. We can also ask God to speak to us. In the deepest places of our doubt, we can come to Him and ask Him to tell us what He wants us to know about our situation. Ask Him what He wants us to know about ourselves. He knows us intimately. He carefully knit us together in our mothers' wombs. He knows our deepest secrets and desires even better than we know (Psalm 139:14-16).

Ask Him to give you supernatural revelation, and then wait for His response. When I ask, the answer does not always come right away. But at some point, God will speak to me through a person, song, sermon, or thought.

How did Gideon respond when God told him that he would save Israel from the hand of the Midianites?

Much in the same way, I fear, I would have. He said, "Who, me? You must be mistaken. My family is poor, and I am the least in my father's house" (Judges 6:15, paraphrased). Gideon did not believe in himself, so he assumed he could not fulfill such a task. Again, Satan was taking advantage of Gideon's vulnerable state by whispering lies that would keep him hidden and defeated.

Something similar happened to me as a new widow and single mom. I believed the lies that I wasn't enough and that being a widow was a reproach. I shrunk back in self-pity and depression. Dispelling the lies took remembering the truth through reading God's Word daily and surrounding myself with Spirit-filled people. Close fellowship with like believers is essential for keeping our minds focused on truth. Although God hasn't sent an angel to speak to me yet, I'm here for it if He ever does!

At first, Gideon was unsure if the angel was from God. He asked for a sign to prove that God was speaking to him. Gideon presented cooked meat from a kid, unleavened cakes, and broth to the angel. The angel told him to lay it all on a rock and pour the broth over it. Gideon obeyed. The angel then took his staff, touched it, and a fire came up out of the rock and consumed it all. After this, the angel disappeared. What an amazing experience! Gideon's remaining doubts that a legitimate angel had a real message from God were gone.

This interaction with God and His angel infused Gideon with new strength and purpose. He came out of hiding and built an altar for the LORD. That same night, God instructed him first to tear down the altar of Baal, which Gideon's father had constructed and then cut down the grove by it. Finally, God instructed Gideon to build an altar for the LORD in its place and use the wood from the grove he cut down to burn an offering on it. Gideon did all of this at night. If anyone had seen him, they would've killed him.

The next morning, the men of the city found out what Gideon had done and called for his death. They told his father, Joash, that he needed to bring Gideon out so that he could be punished. Although Joash was the one who built the altar to Baal in the first place, he defended Gideon and even challenged the men to consult their god, Baal, and let him deal with Gideon. The Bible doesn't specifically tell us, but it makes me wonder if God had also reminded Joash of the truth and to return to Him.

The rest of Gideon's story is fascinating. We see God raise up Gideon as a mighty warrior who successfully delivers the Israelites from their enemies. Even with this, God ensured Gideon understood it was God's power, not his own, that would bring victory by shrinking Gideon's army from 32,000 to 300 men. Meanwhile, the Midianite's army "lay along in the valley like grasshoppers for multitude; and their camels were without number, as the sand by the seaside for multitude" (Judges 7:12). God did not want Israel to "vaunt themselves against" Him, saying, "Mine own hand hath saved me" (Judges 7:2). He wanted them to know it was God that saved them.

Esther

Esther is another example of God choosing someone we wouldn't have expected. Growing up in Persia, Esther was an average Jewish girl. An orphan cared for by her cousin, Mordecai, Esther was not remarkable according to worldly standards, yet God would use her to save an entire nation from genocide.

After banishing Queen Vashti, King Ahasuerus (Xerxes 1) sought a new wife. He instructed his servants to gather young maidens from his kingdom's provinces. After a set time of purification, each maiden was presented to the king. Esther "obtained grace and favor" above all the other women and was made queen of Persia (Esther 2:17).

I can imagine how Esther would have felt completely overwhelmed by her sudden transition into such a high position. She went from being a poor orphan girl to the most important woman in Persia. Even so, Esther retained her humility and appreciation for her family. She continued to respect and obey her guardian, Mordecai, and agreed to keep her Jewish identity a secret.

Around this time, King Ahasuerus promoted one of his princes, Haman, to the second-highest seat and commanded everyone to bow to his new right-hand man. Mordecai refused to bow down or give reverence to Haman. When the king's servants asked him why he would not show reverence to Haman, Mordecai didn't answer, but I believe he loved God and knew He alone was worthy of worship. However, Mordecai's refusal to bow down angered Haman, and he determined to destroy not only Mordecai but also his people, the Jews.

When Mordecai discovered Haman's plot for the Jews' destruction, he went to Esther and asked her to plead with the king for help. At first, Esther said no. Back then, it was unlawful for anyone, even the queen, to enter the inner court to speak with the king unless they were called. The punishment for showing up unrequested was death unless the king granted permission by extending a golden scepter. It had been 30 days since the king had called Esther, so an attempt to speak to the king without an invitation would put her in serious peril.

Mordecai had great faith in God and trusted that He would save His people. He told Esther that deliverance would come to the Jews, with or without her, but what if she were placed in the kingdom for such a time as this?

Mordecai's words provide an excellent reminder that God's plans will come to pass. Whether we're obedient or not, God will have His way. I would not want to miss my opportunity to be a part of the story God is weaving! Esther did not want this either. She requested that all the Jews in Shushan and her maidens fast for three days and nights. After this time of prayer and fasting, she would go to the king. Esther was not confident of the outcome but was willing to be obedient and courageously said, "If I perish, I perish" (Esther 4:16).

Esther did obtain favor in the king's sight, and he held out the golden scepter to her. She requested a banquet for her, the king, and Haman. During the banquet, she revealed Haman's evil plot, but Haman had already tricked King Ahasuerus into sealing with his ring the decree to have all Jews destroyed. Unfortunately, once sealed, a ruling could not be reversed; however, the king granted the Jews permission to gather and stand for their lives. He proclaimed that they could destroy, slay, and cause to perish all the power of the people and province that would assault them (Esther 8:11). Ultimately, the Jews fought back and were not destroyed.

God elevated Esther from an unknown orphan to a woman of influence and power. She used her position to help her people even though it could've meant her destruction. Because of her bravery and selflessness, she will always be honored and remembered.

The Book of Esther exemplifies the importance of the truth, particularly when stressful situations challenge our beliefs. She had Mordecai, who spoke words of encouragement and purpose over her. Of course, they did not have the Bible back then, so they needed one another to pass down the memories of what God had done and Who He was. We are fortunate to have God's Word today, but we still need to hear the truths in its pages proclaimed over us by others in our lives, especially in those hard places when grief and fear threaten us.

Once reminded of the truth, we have a choice. We can oppose God's calling for us or lock in on Him and follow where He leads. We can do this with confidence and courage, knowing He is near, and His purposes always come to pass.

Heavenly Father,
We confess to you that we often forget the truth of your Word. We confess that oftentimes we listen to lies the enemy whispers to us. Thank you, Lord, for not leaving us defenseless. Thank you for reminding us of the truth of who You created us to be. You never meant for us to live this life alone. You created us for fellowship. We are so grateful for friends who encourage us when we need it. You set the lonely in families and lead

out the prisoners with singing. Thank you for freeing us to be the people you created us to be! Fill us daily with Your grace and Spirit so we can live out Your purpose for our lives. We love you!

In Jesus Name,

Amen

Chapter 10

Death

No one likes to talk about death. We don't like to think about it either, which is ironic since death is the one sure thing we can all count on. No one is making it out of here alive! All of us will die. There's no diet, exercise program, pill, or medical treatment that will prevent anyone from dying. Of course, we all know this, but the finality and mystery of death are strong enough to make us want to avoid it for as long as possible.

God built us this way. Our very being craves life. God made us to live. Jesus came to give us life—not just any life, but an abundant life (John 10:10). He created us in His image, and He is eternal. Just as He lives forever, so will we live forever. Our souls are eternal.

Did you know that scientists have discovered a flash of light at the moment of conception?[18]

Jesus said, "I am the light of the world. He who follows Me shall not walk in darkness but have the light of life" (John 8:12).

"This then is the message we have heard of Him, and declare unto you, that God is light, and in Him is no darkness at all" (1 John 1:5).

"And the city had no need of the sun, neither of the moon, to shine in it: for the glory of God did lighten it, and the Lamb is the light thereof" (Revelation 21:23).

Again, we are made in His image, so it fascinates me to think about a burst of light at our conception! In his book *Imagine Heaven*, John Burke chronicles multiple testimonies of those who have had a near-death experience (NDE), wherein someone comes to the brink of death or dies and, after recovery, recounts an out-of-body experience of encountering Heaven. Burke identifies several similarities every NDE'er shared in their experiences. One is about light.

Those who return commonly claim that the light was brighter than the sun but did not hurt their eyes. They could look directly into it. Also, every being they encountered, including Jesus, was made of light. Light emanated from them. Their assertions certainly match the truth of Scripture, but even those who were not believers, never having read or heard the Bible preached, made this same declaration.[19]

How exciting to think that our light shines into eternity when our hearts cease to beat! The light created at the very beginning of our existence never dims; it's within us forever.

What if we talked about death like this? A transition from this temporary world where we see darkness and brokenness to a world we were created to inhabit forever, with light that never dims and all being whole and perfect.

Would it still be a subject people avoided? Maybe.

Would it still be a scary mystery that we tried to put off as long as we could? Probably.

The unknown is always somewhat daunting. However, it is possible that the more we study God's Word, the more time we spend with Him in prayer, the more we seek Him and His righteousness, the more familiar we will become with eternal things, and the less fear we'll experience at the thought of what happens next. Those who know Jesus and trust Him know that death is not the end. We have an assurance of a home awaiting us.

After washing His disciples' feet, Jesus shares with them this beautiful promise:

> "Let not your hearts be troubled: ye believe in God, believe also in me. In my Father's house are many mansions: if it were not so, I would have told you. I go to prepare a place for you. And if I go and prepare a

place for you, I will come again, and receive you unto myself; that where I am, there ye may be also. And whither I go ye know, and the way ye know" (John 14:1-4).

Jesus explained that He had to leave, and the news grieved their hearts. They loved Jesus and did not want Him to go. He was their life, and they had given up everything to follow Him. What would they do without him?

We have the same feelings when faced with losing a loved one. Our life is bound up in theirs, and we can't imagine continuing without them. The fear that we won't be okay creeps in because of how much we love and depend on them.

But Jesus consoled them with these words: "And I will pray the Father, and He shall give you another Comforter, that he may abide with you forever.... I will not leave you comfortless: I will come to you" (John 14:16,18).

He promised that although He would not walk beside them each day, He would still be with them through the Holy Spirit, the Comforter. He even says that the Comforter would allow them to do "greater works" than the works He did because He is going to His Father (John 14:12).

What a powerful promise! Jesus would live and work within them in a mightier way than He was at the time. We have the same promise with the same Spirit dwelling within us.

What about our loved ones? Are they still living in us when their hearts stop beating and their physical bodies die? While not in the same way that the Holy Spirit dwells within us, the life they had and their investments in others continue to live on through us.

My husband left behind a legacy of generosity, love, and industriousness that I see in our children and myself. He modeled a life rooted in Godly principles and a heart for helping others. The example he set and the life he lived will be passed down through our children, grandchildren, and great-grandchildren. His life mattered, and he made a difference. That will never change.

When our loved ones go to their forever homes, the life they had here lives on through the ones they leave behind. We will carry them with us until the day we join them. And what a glorious day that will be! We will be reunited and experience Jesus face-to-face together (1 Corinthians 13:12).

A Biblical Perspective on Death

Solomon was the wisest and richest man to ever live. God chose him to be king after his father, David. Humbled by this great responsibility, Solomon prayed to receive wisdom and knowledge to judge God's people rightly. God was pleased with Solomon's selfless request, which was more concerned with carrying out his God-given responsibilities than anything for himself, like wealth, honor, or longevity. His main desire was to steward the tasks God laid before him.

Along with granting him wisdom, God also bestowed upon Solomon great riches, wealth, and honor that exceeded any king then and to come (I Kings 1-3).

We can, therefore, look to Solomon for a proper perspective of death. Solomon tells us that the day of death is better than the day of birth (Ecclesiastes 7:1). He goes on to say that it is better to go to the house of mourning than to the house of feasting (Ecclesiastes 7:2). That certainly flies in the face of what makes sense to us! I don't know about you, but I'd much rather go to a party than a funeral and witness a birth over a death. But here, Solomon is telling us differently.

Solomon had everything this world could offer: riches beyond the wealthiest billionaires today and thousands of women. Nothing was beyond his grasp. However, he admits that all of it was vanity and vexation of spirit (Ecclesiastes 1:14). Despite receiving his insight, we continue to think we'd be happy to have more money, vacation time, friends, and possessions. Life would be perfect. Why do we think that?

I think the answer lies in the Tenth Commandment: do not covet. We see what everyone else has and decide we need that, too. We are disappointed, thinking we can't be happy without those things. The truth is those things don't fill us because we were not made for them. We were created to know God and to worship Him alone. When we set up and worship these other idols, they always fall short.

Accordingly, we have the wisest man in the world's history telling us the truth. He *did* have it all, and it *did not* bring him satisfaction or happiness. He says that whatsoever his eyes desired, he apprehended, and when he looked around at all he had achieved and collected, all of it was "vexation of spirit," "vanity," and "no profit under the sun" (Ecclesiastes 2:4-11).

I've experienced thinking I'd be happy, at peace, and satisfied when I obtained that job, house, car, or goal. However, over and over again, I've attained those goals and realized the truth of Solomon's words. Even while writing this book, the sensation has hit me.

Publishing a book has been my dream since I was a little girl. I've always loved reading and imagined how wonderful it would be to become an author who could move others with words by conveying ideas and stories to inspire and entertain. I'm finally doing that, but no matter how many books I publish, the outcome will never deliver the joy and completion my heart seeks. The excitement and satisfaction will always be temporary.

Solomon said there is a season for everything, and God wants us to do good in this life and enjoy the good of all our labors (Ecclesiastes 3). However, we must keep the proper perspective to know that everything we have and do here is for a season and not meant to last forever.

Some seasons are harder to say goodbye to than others. Sometimes, I think it would be perfect if we could have summer all year long, but I've learned to find good in every season: the cold, dark ones and the warm, lighthearted ones. This applies to seasons in our lives as well.

We will not feel complete and experience continual peace and joy in this life, only in the life to come. Maybe this is why Solomon said that the day we die is better than the day we're born. On the day we die, we arrive in the life to come without sorrow, pain, or death, and God will wipe away all our tears (Revelation 21:4).

Until then, I believe He sees and holds each of our tears. His compassion is so great, His love for us so immense, that He holds us in our sorrow even now. With sorrow comes mourning, but Solomon said it is better to mourn than to feast. He even says sorrow is better than laughter, for the heart is made better by the sadness of the countenance (Ecclesiastes 7:2-3). When in sorrow, we understand our great need for God.

> "Whatever else might be the reason for our disappointments, there is no question that God uses them to draw us to Himself. To wean our hearts from every other perceived source of life so that we might come to find our life in Him."[20]

I have grown and learned much more in times of great trial and sorrow than in easy, happier times. My spirit longs for Jesus in the trials. Books will collect dust, riches will fade away, and our bodies will grow frail. However, our spirits will grow bigger and stronger, preparing for our ultimate purpose: to completely conform to Christ's image and live with Him forever!

Psalm 116:15 tells us that the death of His saints is precious in the sight of God. God knows the great joy, peace, love, and light we'll experience through death! We are precious to Him. We certainly do experience God now through His Spirit, but we only "see through a glass darkly." God delights in the fact that we will see Him face-to-face in our death! We will know as we are known (1 Corinthians 13:12).

The Apostle Paul says it this way; "We are confident, I say, and willing rather to be absent from the body, and to be present with the Lord" (2 Corinthians 5:8).

Isn't it interesting how he uses the phrase "absent from the body?" That's what death means. It's not an ending or darkness; it's a transition or movement to another place. We'll leave our bodies behind and immediately find ourselves in the presence of the Lord. The One we have loved and served from a distance for so many years will finally be right before us.

Have you ever imagined what it must have been like to walk with Jesus when he lived on earth? I think about the disciples and how amazing it would have been to be included in His inner circle. They got to eat with Him and hear from Him every day. They could ask Him questions at any time. We have the same privileges today, but they saw Him in the flesh! Oh, to be in the crowd watching as he passed by or enjoying a meal with Him! I think about looking at Him and immediately feeling His love and peace. That's what Heaven will be like! We'll be with Him—our Father, Creator, Savior, and Friend.

Why Did Jesus Weep?

If the death of His saints is precious to the Lord, then why did He weep at the tomb of His friend Lazarus (John 11: 1-45)? Jesus loved Lazarus and his sisters, Mary and Martha. When Lazarus got sick, Mary and Martha called for Jesus immediately, confident he could and would heal their brother and Jesus' dear friend. However, Jesus delayed, and by the time He arrived, Lazarus was dead. The sisters were devastated. Martha rebuked Jesus, telling Him that Lazarus would not have died if He had only been there. I think all of us can understand how Martha felt. When a loved one passes, we wonder where God is and why He didn't save them. It doesn't make sense to us, and it didn't make sense to Martha.

Then Jesus wept. Some say He wept because of His friends' lack of faith in Him. They were disappointed in Jesus for not arriving to save their brother and friend in time. They did not know that Jesus planned to do something even greater than healing a sick man. He had plans to demonstrate His power over death!

Jesus said, "This sickness is not unto death, but for the glory of God, that the Son of God might be glorified thereby" (John 11:4).

How often do we focus on the circumstances before us and forget to look for God in them? We fail to consider that He might be working in the very moment when we feel like He is the furthest away. This is how Mary and Martha felt: Jesus was far away and missed His opportunity to help them. However, Jesus was working then to do something even greater than they could have imagined. They wanted to see a miracle of healing, but Jesus wanted to show them a greater miracle: a resurrection!

What a wonderful lesson for us to remember! When Jesus doesn't "arrive" in time to answer our prayer, He may be preparing to do something even bigger and more glorious than we can imagine!

Others say he wept out of compassion, seeing their great sorrow and grief. This also makes sense, for Jesus dearly loved His friends.

A friend offered a different perspective, one I had never heard before. After he pulled up beside me in the parking lot at my daughter's school, I shared how, earlier that morning, I had been grieving over the death of a young mother in our community. Along with my sorrow, I also expressed the questions I had been asking God. Why didn't God save her? Why didn't He prevent the circumstances that led to her death?

My friend then relayed a dream God had given to him for comfort after losing his only daughter, a young, single mom. As a believer, he rejoiced in knowing she was with her Savior; however, as a dad, he grieved and wondered why God would take her so soon, leaving her son without his mom. He struggled to align his faith with his longing to understand why. In the dream, God revealed to my friend that Jesus wept at Lazarus' tomb because He knew He was getting ready to call Lazarus out of paradise. Lazarus was perfectly whole and happy, and Jesus was about to bring him back to a broken world. This grieved Jesus.

My friend felt so much peace knowing that even if his

daughter had the choice, she would not want to return. She was home. As a dad, he wanted the best for his daughter, and pulling her out of paradise would not be in her best interests. Would it be better for him? Of course, but not for her. He and his wife now have the privilege of raising their grandson and seeing her legacy and spirit live on in him.

I left the school parking lot that day praising God and thanking Him for hearing my cries that morning and answering me. God used this dear man to comfort my heart.

A Different View of Death

When we married, my husband and I promised to love each other "'til death do us part." It is a common vow made at weddings, but how many of us truly understand what it denotes? For me, the pledge brought to mind images of two elderly people saying goodbye in a hospital bed surrounded by children, grandchildren, and great-grandchildren. Never did I imagine that the day death came to part us would be any sooner!

We assume people will live into their 70s or 80s; some lucky ones will reach their 90s. Psalm 90:10 says, "The days of our years are threescore (60) and ten; and if by reason of strength they be fourscore (80) years, yet is their strength labor and sorrow; for it is soon cut off, and we fly away." There you go! We're meant to live 70 years; if we're lucky, we'll reach 80.

Would your life look any different if you knew you were guaranteed a solid 80 years? Would you throw caution to the wind more often, certain that no sickness, accident, or disease will result in a premature end? Would you put off pursuing God, deciding you had plenty of time to "get right with God"?

What about your spiritual life? Would you live each day focused on the eternal? Or would you decide to wait until you got up in age before considering eternal things?

If we agree that God uniquely created and designed each person for a special purpose, why do we assume our lifespans should all be the same?

If you're like me, you don't usually think about dying. It's unpleasant to think about, and death is just not supposed to happen until we're old and gray.

What if we thought about death like we think about birth? We look forward to a new baby with excitement. We plan for his/her arrival for months. Our thoughts are filled with hopes and dreams over a new life and its promises.

We can think about death with similar anticipation of the new life we will experience in Heaven—a life far richer and more rewarding than anything we've experienced in our natural lives, where the beauty, joy, peace, and love we experience now are a mere foreshadowing of what's to come.

It's one thing to talk about our homegoing, yet it's quite different to think about the homegoing of the ones we love. When loved ones enter their forever home, fear creeps in because we depend on them for security, joy, and peace. How will we be okay without them? We lament the lost opportunities and joys they will never experience because their lives were "cut short." What if all those lost opportunities are just plastic trinkets compared to what they'll experience in Heaven? Instead of looking at it as a life "cut short," we could see it as a beginning—a life full of wonder and beauty that pales compared to anything we've ever known. They are the lucky ones who have finally arrived home, the place for which they were created.

Knowing all this will certainly not erase our sorrow and grief. As Christians, our grief is mixed with hope and joy. The emotions do co-exist! I had difficulty understanding this in the beginning.

I tend to be a perfectionist and a people-pleaser. I want to do everything perfectly the first time, even when it's something I've never done before, including this devastating loss. I felt like everyone was watching me to see how I'd handle my circumstances.

While so confused by the onslaught of emotions and overwhelmed by the number of decisions I needed to make, I didn't want to do it wrong! On the one hand, I was dealing with the devastating ruins that were now my life; on the other, I was also wondering if I was grieving correctly!

For instance, I wondered when was it okay to feel happy again? If too soon, did that mean I didn't love him as much as I should have? Or, if it was taking too long, was there something wrong with me, and I needed serious mental help? I was an emotional wreck, thinking that something was wrong with me because other people probably did much better at this than how I was doing. The worst part was feeling so ashamed of my thoughts and emotions that I didn't talk to anyone about them. Not even God.

I pulled myself up by my bootstraps and marched ahead, pretending to be strong and put together. People would constantly comment on how strong I was, and I would start crying inside, wanting to scream, "No! I am not strong and am only doing what I have to do to survive." Of course, I didn't say that. I just replied, "Thank you."

I was wrong to keep my confusion and anger stuffed down. The healing began when I started to open up to God with the depths of my pain and questions. I heard Susie Larson, author and speaker, say, "You have to feel to heal." Once I allowed those feelings to surface and come out, God poured in with healing revelation and truth. I learned that my feelings were *not* "wrong." The only "wrong" was worrying about how I appeared to other people. Focusing on Jesus, not other people, was the answer.

Jesus taught me that I didn't have to choose joy over grief. I could have them both, even simultaneously. Yes, I would feel the pain of being separated from my other half, but at the same time, I would feel joy for his victory—joy in knowing that Rob had finished his race and realized his greatest reward: seeing Jesus face to face. The two conditions—grief and joy—are both/and, not either/or.

It's normal to experience intense sorrow when some-one dies. There is no "right" way to grieve or a timeline in which to do it.

Are other people going to judge you? Probably. We live in a fallen world, remember? However, God will not judge you. He loves you so much and will walk with you and comfort you. Other people's judgments don't matter.

I've heard it said, "The greater the grief, the greater the love." Amid this great grief, we can remember that it's because of our great privilege to love and be loved. Grief and joy together again!

How exciting to consider that the most amazing moments in our lives will pale compared to what God has prepared for us! Those wonderful mountaintop experiences never last here on this earth, but Heaven promises one never-ending mountaintop experience. Paul's prayer for the church at Ephesus was that they would be able to comprehend the breadth, length, depth, and height of the love Christ has for them

(Ephesians 3:18-19). We catch glimpses of that here, but we'll know His love fully there.

The Ultimate Vacation

Imagine that you have planned the trip of a lifetime. You are going to Bora Bora (or insert the most perfect and peaceful place you can imagine) for two weeks. Months before your departure, you're already anticipating the freedom from stress and peace that will surround you. You envision magnificent sunsets, delicious food, and hours spent exploring the colorful coral reefs and lush green mountains with the people you love the most. You can already feel the warm sun on your face and the soft, white sand between your toes. You dream about the abundant time you'll have to rest and relax.

The days and weeks leading up to your departure are filled with planning and organizing so life can go on as usual while you're away. Arrangements will be made for the pets, someone must collect the mail, cover for you at work, etc. All the while, your mind cannot stop thinking about the moment your plane touches down and you take that first step into your perfect oasis. Sometimes, you just can't contain the excitement and feel like it may burst out of you at any minute. You cannot wait!

The day comes, and just as you walk out the door, someone stops you and says, "No, wait! You can't go. I need you here. I'll be lost without you." Would you stay? Of course not! You've been planning and dreaming about this day for quite some time. You've made all of the arrangements. You know your loved one will be okay.

You're floating as you board the plane. It won't be long now, and you'll be there! At long last, you're on your way! The plane takes off smoothly.

Suddenly, however, the cabin gets dark. You look out the window and can't see anything. The plane has been enveloped in clouds. As the pilot instructs everyone to be seated and secure their seatbelts, you feel yourself being jostled from side to side. *Oh no*, you think. Maybe this wasn't such a good idea after all. You're scared and wonder if all the days and months of dreaming and planning were worthwhile if it ended like this! In that instant, you forget about everything else and see only death and destruction.

However, the shaking soon subsides. The clouds clear, and an endless blue sky stretches before you. All is right again.

Finally, you arrive, and it's not like you imagined. It's a hundred times better! Everything you read and heard from others was nowhere close. Your heart swells with gratitude to be in such a fantastic place. The terror you felt just hours before is forgotten.

Your two weeks end, and you don't want to leave! How could you possibly leave such a perfect place? You think about everything waiting for you at home and decide it all seems dismal and unimportant compared to where you are now.

What if we thought about eternity in terms of getting ready for an epic vacation like this? And what if we lived every day in preparation for that trip? What would our lives look like if we invested our time, energy, and resources into our family and community to prepare them for our absence and their arrival into that perfect eternal destination? When our time comes to go home, those we leave behind will be comforted with the knowledge that we are in paradise, enjoying our final reward with our Creator. They will be left with hope and anticipation of the day when it will be their turn, and we will be reunited!

As I said earlier, the joy of knowing will be mixed with sorrow over their absence. We will miss them tremendously, but we will not be broken, hopeless, or destroyed. We will be sustained in knowing that we're heading in the same direction to join them soon, arriving safely in Jesus' arms.

However, for now, He still has work for us to do. Let this give us renewed energy and purpose as we prepare for that glorious day!

Heavenly Father,

We know you have prepared a place for us and are coming again to receive us unto yourself. Thank you, Jesus! Thank you for the hope of Heaven! Thank you for overcoming death and taking its sting. Because of You, death is not a loss; rather, it's a victory! You sought us and bought us with Your redeeming blood. You are our Savior, and our home with You is waiting for us. Thank you for comforting those who mourn and for Your great compassion for us. You know how it hurts to be separated from the ones we love. Thank you that it is only a temporary separation! We long to see You face to face. We long to be with You, Lord. We look forward to that day. Help us, Father, to use our time here to love others as You love them and to see others as You see them. Help us to comfort one another with Your

Words. We love You!

In Jesus Name,

Amen.

Chapter 11

Now What?

I confess that I don't have all the answers. I don't understand many of the whys and hows in this life, but I am sure of my trust in Jesus. I love Him with all my heart, and I know, beyond a shadow of a doubt, that He is good and trustworthy. He is good even when everything around us is far from good. Of course, we praise Him when the outcomes are favorable. We always claim God is good when the disease is healed, the trip is safe, and the healthy baby is born. All good things come from the Father of Lights.

"Every good gift and every perfect gift is from above, and cometh down from the Father of lights, with whom is no variableness, neither shadow of turning" (James 1:17). But God is still good in the dark, where sadness and confusion reign. His character never changes. Where God is, there is goodness. Evil exists in the absence of God; in the absence of light, there is darkness.

God is also good in His judgment and justice. We've all seen what happens when children are left to themselves and receive no consequences for their actions. "For thus saith the LORD that created the heavens; God himself that formed the earth and made it; he hath established it, he created it not in vain, he formed it to be inhabited: I am the LORD; and there is none else. I have not spoken in secret, in a dark place of the earth: I said not unto the seed of Jacob, Seek ye me in vain: I the LORD speak righteousness, I declare things that are right" (Isaiah 45:18-19).

I'm reminded of God's goodness in nature. In the winter, everything looks dead, but if you look closely, you can see the beginnings of buds ready to open with life at the first hint of spring. During a storm, the sky is dark and ominous, but the sun shines just behind it, and at the first break in the clouds, a stream of light will burst through.

God is like this. He is always there, especially in the darkness. He has promised that He is near the brokenhearted and saves the crushed in spirit (Psalms 34:18-19). Nevertheless, it takes a concentrated effort to fix our eyes on Jesus and not let the difficult circumstances defeat or depress us. I wish this were easy for me. It's not. Remembering that I do not have the full picture requires a conscious effort.

God sees everything from the beginning to the end. While I can and do trust in His goodness and sovereignty, I must keep my mind focused on this truth. I do this by immersing myself in His Word, spending time with Him in prayer, and staying close to others who can strengthen and encourage me as we worship and praise Him together.

Renewing My Mind

One day, while I was running a quick grocery store errand, the Lord showed me how easy it is to focus on the natural and overlook what the Holy Spirit is doing. After grabbing my items, I headed to the front, looking for the shortest line. If I'm honest, I usually race from one thing to the next, telling myself I'm being efficient with my time. I found a line with one person and hurried to wait behind her.

After a few minutes, I realized a problem had erupted, and this probably wasn't the shortest line after all. I started looking for another line but overheard the cashier explain to the customer that her food stamps did not cover a particular item in her cart. The woman reached behind her little girl to remove the item from her buggy. At that moment, I felt the Holy Spirit urging me to help her. She needed only a small amount to pay the difference.

This situation convicted me of my tendency to focus

on myself and my agenda rather than asking the Holy Spirit for eyes to see others as Jesus sees them. When I focus on myself and my world, I get wrapped up in all the places I feel are lacking and begin to feel sorry for myself. I also start striving to "fix" all the problems in my life.

The incident in the grocery store reminded me to lift my eyes and be attentive to what other people need. It also reminded me to constantly communicate with God so that I am ready to be led by the Holy Spirit in every circumstance. Although adherence isn't easy, relief and joy always result when I transfer my attention to others instead of myself.

A friend once told me, "God can't pour in more blessings until we give away what we have." This is true for both physical and spiritual blessings. He repeatedly fills and refills me, but I must give away the love God has lavished on me. Proverbs 11:25 says, "A generous person will prosper; whoever refreshes others will be refreshed." The more I relinquish the gifts I've received, the more gifts God lavishes on me!

This tendency to rush from one thing to another usually occurs because I've created a jam-packed schedule with no margin. Margin leaves room in my schedule to be available when God calls me to a particular opportunity. I may think I'm being productive with a full schedule, but I fall into a mindset of focusing inward with no room for others' needs. By slowing down and foregoing the urge to fill every minute of my day, I can identify and welcome opportunities to serve and love others as they arise.

The greatest commandment tells us to love the Lord our God with all our hearts, souls, and minds and to love our neighbor as ourselves (Matthew 26: 36-40).

Closing Thoughts

In the beginning, I hated for anyone to call me a widow. I knew at the time how ridiculous that was because I was indeed a widow. The title just made what had happened that much more real. I was still in shock and felt so numb, and it took a few months for the reality that he was gone to sink in. Yes, I was a widow. I had just lost my identity as a wife and was trying to find a new identity; I knew that being a widow was not it! I was stuck in a place where I had to figure out who I was.

My perspective changed the day a friend told me that the moment my husband died, Jesus Himself stepped in to be my children's Father and my Husband. Jesus gives special favor and honor to widows and orphans, she said. Because my grief was so dark and consuming in the beginning, I did not see this, but she was right. Jesus was incredibly patient and kind by meeting me where I was. He comforted me and took care of us all. I saw His hand in every aspect of life: in friends, strangers, and the quiet times I spent with Him.

I now know exactly who I am. I am God's image bearer. I am a child of God. I am a peculiar treasure to Him. All the titles I used to identify myself with—widow, wife, mom, sister, teacher, business owner—are roles I have now or once had. They don't define me. God does.

We are all God's children. He has a particular purpose and plan for each of our lives and gives each of us an identity to live out.

Have you asked Him who He created you to be? Have you asked Him to reveal His divine purpose for your life?

Ask Him what He calls you.

God has given me gifts to help others, calling me a healer and counselor. With my God-given identity, I am excited to walk into this role and anticipate how God will use me in this next season of my life.

By sharing my journey and what I learned, I pray that I will encourage and provide hope to anyone grieving and questioning God's goodness.

I also pray that my words have lifted Jesus so you can see Him working in your life and your story.

He is good.

Heavenly Father,

You are the King of Kings and Lord of Lords. Hallowed be Thy Name. Thy Kingdom come, Thy will be done! You are the First and the Last. You are the Creator of Heaven and Earth, and all that's in them. We could never come to a complete understanding of Your Being and Your Power. You are perfect in all Your ways and holy in all Your works. Your will is perfect. You are not only good, but You are good personified. How grateful we are to be Your children and to be loved by You. Lord, mold us into Your Image. Create in us a clean heart. Draw us to You and fill us daily with Your Holy Spirit. We want to serve You faithfully. We love You and praise You!

In Jesus Name,

Amen

Endnotes

1. "grief." *Webstersdictionary1828.com*. 2024. https://www.webstersdictionary1828.com/Dictionary/grief. (4 November 2024).

2. "oppress." *Webstersdictionary1828.com*. 2024. https://www.webstersdictionary1828.com/Dictionary/grief. (4 November 2024).

3. Lewis, C.S. (1898-1963). A Grief Observed. Harper San Fransisco, 2001.

4. Balasek, K. (2022, September 7). *Widows Are Younger Than You Think*. Www.Rethinking65.com. Retrieved November 4, 2024, from https://rethinking65.com/widows-are-younger-than-you-think/#:~:text=There%20are%2011.8%20million%20widows,of%20younger%20widows%20could%20climb.

5. Burke, J. (2015). *Imagine Heaven*. Baker Books.

6. Hart, Joseph. (1759). Come, Ye Sinners, Poor and Needy. https://sovereigngracemusic.com/music/songs/come-ye-sinners-poor-and-needy/

7. Ten Boom, C. (2006). *The Hiding Place*. Chosen Books.

8. Luther, Martin. (2000) The Complete Sermons of Martin Luther, Volume 2.

9. Elliot, E. (2013). *Passion and Purity: Learning to Bring Your Love Life Under Christ's Control*. Revell.

10. Philippe, J. (2007). *Interior Freedom*. Scepter Pubs.

11. Van Zeller, H. (2015). *The Mystery of Suffering*. Christian Classics.

12. Henderson, K. D. (n.d.). I *Would Have Pulled Joseph Out*. Learning to Live For His Glory. https://kdhenderson.wordpress.com/i-would-have-pulled-joseph-out/#:~:text=Nor%20is%20it%20about%20standing,responded%2C%20"Trust%20 Me."&text=Kimberly-,I%20would%20have%20 pulled%20Joseph,Out%20of%20that%20pit.

13. "good." *Webstersdictionary1828.com*. 2024. https://www.webstersdictionary1828.com/Dictionary/grief. (4 November 2024).

14. Lewis, C. (2001). *Mere Christianity*. Harper San Francisco.

15. Michelangelo. AZQuotes.com, Wind and Fly LTD, 2025. https://www.azquotes.com/quote/722675, accessed January 27, 2025.

16. Lewis, C. (2001). The Weight of Glory (1st ed.). Harper One.

17. Carroll, L. (1993). *Alice in Wonderland.* Dover Publications.

18. Crew, B. (2016, April 27). *Scientists Just Captured The Flash of Light That Sparks When a Sperm Meets an Egg.* Www.Sciencealert.com. Retrieved November 10, 2024, from https://www.sciencealert.com/scientists-just-captured-the-actual-flash-of-light-that-sparks-when-sperm-meets-an-egg

19. Burke, J. (2015). *Imagine Heaven.* Baker Books.

20. Eldredge, J. (2016). *Walking with God: How to Hear His Voice.* Thomas Nelson.

About the Author

Kim Kiser is a widow and the mother of seven children. After graduating from the University of Georgia with a Bachelor of Science in Education, she taught school for five years. In 1997, Kim transitioned to homeschooling her children and later started a small business.

She has a deep love for God's Word and is passionate about inspiring others to develop their own love for the Bible. Kim lives in Georgia with her three daughters and two dogs. An avid reader, you can often find her in her backyard, book in hand, with her bare feet in the grass, enjoying the sunshine.

www.ingramcontent.com/pod-product-compliance
Lightning Source LLC
Chambersburg PA
CBHW071410090426
42737CB00011B/1409